I learned more American history from the Congress project than from any other course I have ever taken.

Everyone hates grammar, but you made a game of it.

I think I got the greatest thrill out of reading and acting out the plays.

I definitely developed an interest in poetry which has continued.

The tomb made math fun and challenging.

What we do in school etches more deeply on our memories and on our lives than the content we studied. Yesterday's word for it was motivation; today's words are *student involvement* and *participation*. Al Cullum calls it "pushing back the desks." He has been doing it for twenty years in elementary schools.

When he asked former students if they remembered his class, letters poured in. We present some excerpts together with descriptions of the projects that gave new directions to young lives.

What happens when Al Cullum pushes back the desks will, we believe, give many educators the inspiration and courage to involve children in creative learning experiences. Cullum is Cullum, but each of us, in his own fashion, can "push back the desks."

WILLIAM D. BOUTWELL
Vice-President
Scholastic Magazines, Inc.

What tortured me in my school days was the fact that the school had not the completeness of the world. It was a special arrangement for giving lessons. It could only be suitable for grownup people who were conscious of the special need of such places and therefore ready to accept their teaching at the cost of disassociation from life. But children are in love with life, and it is their first love. All its color and movement attract their eager attention. Are we quite sure of our wisdom in stifling this love?

RABINDRANATH TAGORE

Push Back the Desks

Albert Cullum

School of Education, Boston University

Citation Press, New York • 1967

Acknowledgments

For reprint permission grateful acknowledgment is made to:

Chappell & Co., Inc., for excerpt from Kurt Weill and Langston Hughes' "Lonely House" from the musical STREET SCENE. Copyright © 1946 by Kurt Weill and Langston Hughes.

Norma Millay Ellis for excerpts from "The Bobolink," copyright 1928, 1955 by Edna St. Vincent Millay and Norma Millay Ellis; "The Fawn," copyright 1934, 1962 by Edna St. Vincent Millay and Norma Millay Ellis; "The Rabbit," copyright 1939, 1967 by Edna St. Vincent Millay and Norma Millay Ellis; all from COLLECTED POEMS OF EDNA ST. VINCENT MILLAY, published by Harper & Row, Publishers.

Harcourt, Brace & World, Inc., for excerpts from THE PEOPLE, YES by Carl Sandburg, copyright 1936 by Harcourt, Brace & World, Inc.; renewed 1964 by Carl Sandburg; and for excerpt from ABRAHAM LINCOLN: THE PRAIRIE YEARS, Volume II by Carl Sandburg.

Holt, Rinehart and Winston, Inc. for three lines from "The Runaway" from COMPLETE POEMS OF ROBERT FROST. Copyright 1923 by Holt, Rinehart and Winston, Inc. Copyright 1951 by Robert Frost.

Alfred A. Knopf, Inc., for "I, Too, Sing America" from SELECTED POEMS BY LANGSTON HUGHES, copyright 1926 by Alfred A. Knopf, Inc., © 1954 by Langston Hughes; and for "Merry-Go-Round" from SELECTED POEMS BY LANGSTON HUGHES, copyright 1942 by Langston Hughes.

The Macmillan Company for excerpt from "The Leaden-Eyed" from COLLECTED POEMS by Vachel Lindsay. Copyright 1914 by The Macmillan Company, renewed 1942 by Elizabeth C. Lindsay; and for excerpt from "Personality" from A TAGORE READER, edited by Amiya Chakravarty, copyright © 1961 by The Macmillan Company.

New Directions Publishing Corporation for excerpts from "The Ballad of the Little Square," "Rider's Song," "Lament for Ignacio Sanchez Majias" from SELECTED POEMS by Federico Garcia Lorca, translated by Stephen Spender and J. L. Gili, copyright 1955 by New Directions.

Harold Ober Associates Inc., for "Old Dog Queenie" and "Brand New Clothes" from THE LANGSTON HUGHES READER, copyright © 1958 by Langston Hughes.

> Front cover photograph by Alfred Porto, Rye, New York: "Doing the *Mikado* without music is fun and a great deal faster if you furnish your own sounds!"
> Inside photographs by Alfred Porto and Diana Beddoe.
> Back cover photograph by TPA, New York City.

2nd printing, April 1971
Printed in the U.S.A.

To the
Children of St. Luke's School, 1948-1955,
and the
Children of the Rye Public Schools, 1956-1966,
who helped me
Push Back the Desks

Contents

Foreword

ONE NEED ONLY LOOK BACK on his own years of schooling to realize that exciting teachers are not common. We learn in the subjects we are required or elect to take because learning itself is rewarding, but in all too many instances, we learn in spite of, rather than because of, our teachers.

Albert Cullum brings to the classroom both vitality and excitement. He is not a conventional teacher, for what his students do or see is generally quite different from what is usual within a school. He is conventional, however, in that he deals with conventional subject matter; his classes are confronted with the basic ingredients of the school program — vocabulary, grammar, the arts, geography, science, the social studies. He takes material in these school areas and infuses it with a vitality that makes it meaningful for students. Mr. Cullum may reject the recommended procedures in a course of study, but he knows what is in it and respects it.

Mr. Cullum's ingenuity as a teacher is not limited to any one level or subject as the many chapters in this book demonstrate, for he can devise for any subject situations in which young learners feel at home and can activate their capacities for learning. His techniques range from the prosaic to the dramatic. He draws considerably upon those with which students are familiar through mass media and which intrigue them — panel discussions, exhibitions, launchings, total environments, trips, and demonstrations. This approach to the material to be learned is always contemporary and exciting.

Most basic, however, is Mr. Cullum's attitude toward the students he teaches. Without exception they have his respect; he sees them as sensitive and aware individuals with ideas to be heard and considered. And in this setting, boys and girls become responsible and hard-working learners.

It is good indeed that Mr. Cullum has taken the time to set down some of his experiences. They should be read widely by teachers of all subjects and of all levels. The book is useful in helping other teachers to use ideas similar to his but invested with their own particular personalities and viewpoints. Mr. Cullum has done the teaching profession a service.

EDWIN ZIEGFELD
Professor of Art and Education
Teachers College, Columbia University
New York City
August 15, 1967

Push Back the Desks

THE OPENING DAY of elementary school is like an opening night on Broadway, with celebrities gathered to look one another over and then to see what the play is all about. As an audience waits expectantly for the opening curtain, so children enter classrooms in September with the hope that something is going to happen. Even the youngsters who don't like school and those who have had little success are secretly hoping that this is the school year when the teacher is not a bore, the year they will be able to laugh together, the year they will be truly accepted.

A sensitive teacher is always aware of the drama inherent in his class. Every class contains a cast ready to play their roles in every subject matter area, and the teacher, sensing the rhythm of his group, soon finds his role too. It is not necessary for the teacher always to play the lead; frequently he can do twice as well in a supporting role. As the school year proceeds, a good teacher will realize that sitting before him, around him, or next to him is a stellar cast!

In his short poem "The Leaden-Eyed," Vachel Lindsay reminds us that:

> Let not young souls be smothered out before
> They do quaint deeds and fully flaunt their pride.
> It is the world's one crime its babes grow dull,
> Its poor are ox-like, limp, and leaden-eyed.
>
> Not that they starve, but starve so dreamlessly,
> Not they they sow, but that they seldom reap,
> Not that they serve, but have no gods to serve,
> Not that they die but that they die like sheep.

I believe elementary schools should be the places where children can "do quaint deeds and fully flaunt their pride." I believe that by exposing children to the excitement and greatness of literature, art, history, geography, and science a passion for learning will develop. I believe that through creative play, imaginative approaches to the curriculum, competitive, yet supportive, games, encouragement of self-expression, and new projects of all sorts children will absorb knowledge and develop the basic skills. I believe that in a relaxed atmosphere, where the teacher respects the individual ability and dignity of each student, and students in turn trust and share with him, learning and teaching are fun for all. I believe that both students and teachers should feel a glow of success at the end of each school project and each school year.

These beliefs have evolved over the twenty years I have taught hundreds of elementary school children. These beliefs have been reinforced time and time again by the enthusiastic responses of students and their parents to my methods of presenting subject matter and teaching basic skills.

The simple gesture of pushing back the desks in a classroom and allowing the natural creative and intellectual drives in children to flow can be the beginning of growth and an understanding of the realities of life. Some of the ways I have pushed back the desks to stimulate the creative and intellectual growth of my students are described in the following chapters. For those who may want to adapt these techniques or to innovate their own, let me answer some questions teachers may raise about the pushing-back-the-desks approach to teaching.

How will children react to new methods of teaching?

I have found that children are interested in two things — *doing* and *doing now*. Children are looking for the unexpected, not the safe; children are looking for noise and laughter, not quiet; children are looking for the heroic, not the common. Everyday, nine to three, should be a *now day* in a child's school life.

Instead of quiet, neatness, and obedient acceptance, let's substitute *eagerness, energy*, and *independence*. Much of the non-school world is a world of great creativity and activity, not a world of conformity and the quiet routine of school workbooks. *Excitement!* That's another key word in a healthy school environment. Excitement can be the stillness that permeates a room when a poem is being read; excitement can be a silent moment of mystery when a new idea is being digested; excitement can be an outburst of laughter. Why can't there be a little mystery, a bit of magic, and a dash of grandeur in elementary classrooms?

Placing class projects on a volunteer basis removes all student fears. I have not yet encountered a class where all students did not volunteer to take part in some aspect of a project. Each child quickly finds his own level of success, and the class works as a team with pride and dignity. Children are supportive of one another. In classroom after classroom I have seen young students more than willing to help one another, to encourage one another, to reassure one another. They are eager to have the thrill of success embrace the entire classroom.

I must admit that I have not been successful with every student. Some found it difficult to be honest with themselves; some had lost complete confidence in themselves to do a really good piece of work, for they had developed a comfortable reliance on workbooks and static recitations. So many, so young, are working for grades rather than becoming involved in the joys of discovering and the joys of learning.

Are young children capable of appreciating great literature, art, or science?

All children have a best foot to put forward and are quite confident of their ability to deal with kings as well as cabbages. Why not expose them to greatness, whether it be the words and thoughts of Shakespeare, Shaw, or Chaucer, a Chagall painting, the mumbo-jumbo sounds of a Vachel Lindsay poem, a Bartok sonata, an intricate math problem, or "big words"?

The elementary school is the perfect place for children to encounter greatness, for they identify readily with great ideas, great personalities, and great emotions, not mediocre ones. I have discovered this to be true of the culturally advantaged and the culturally disadvantaged. Poetry, drama, philosophy, history, and science can be interpreted on all levels; the giants of the world have a definite place in elementary school classrooms, libraries, and hallways. Children respond to them for they have a keen appreciation of the heroic and an exuberant sense of humor.

The sense of greatness and magic that children seek is emotional involvement with subject matter. They are interested in the dramatic developments of a country, the joys and sufferings of a poet, a play or book full of intrigue, and most of all they associate themselves with famous people through role-playing. In my experience, when children are involved and challenged by a subject, they understand the reasons for acquiring the basic skills of reading, writing, and arithmetic and are stimulated to develop these skills.

What will parents and the community say?

I made every effort to involve the family in all my projects. I want parents to share the excitement of a project through discussion and encouragement at home and by attending all open functions of the class. For instance, when students gave lectures on Renoir and conducted geography panels, it was important to them to have the community interested in their presentations; the poetry readings in the assembly needed parents. Every project in which a student stepped off on his own became a more successful project when the community too became involved.

But doesn't a teacher need special training and special skills to initiate new ways and means of teaching and learning?

A teacher need not be a professional actor, musician, artist, or scientist to present greatness to his students. He need only be aware of the creativity and excitement of the outside world and strive to bring that world into his classroom. If a teacher can show a principal the possible structure of a new project and the rules and regulations that will govern it, most administrators will agree to let him try the program. It will be a rewarding experience and not as difficult as it may sound.

Perhaps the most essential quality for a classroom teacher is a sense of humor. Laughter is an important ingredient in a relaxed elementary school atmosphere. Depending on his own personality and style, a teacher can even make the effort to appear absurd at times. For instance, try bursting into song once in a while, dress up and join the Halloween Parade, eat candy in class and share it with the students, or speak with a British, French, or Japanese accent for a bit of variety. It is refreshing when students and teachers can laugh together.

I also believe a teacher should remain a novice and never become an expert in any area of elementary school work. To remain a beginner — to abolish the teacher-authority image — is the first step to seeing truly the students sitting before you. Rainer Maria Rilke, the

German poet, wrote a message all teachers can take to heart:

> Always when you begin to work you must recreate this first innocence, you must return to the ingenuous place where the Angel discovered you when he brought you the first binding message; you must find once more the couch behind the briars where you were then asleep. This time you will not sleep there; you will have to pray and groan . . . no matter, if the Angel deigns to appear, it will be because you have convinced him, not by tears, but your humble resolve to be always beginning . . . to be a Beginner.

When I first began teaching, there was Al Cullum the teacher and Al Cullum the person. I soon discovered that this split personality was not a healthy one for the children nor for me. I realized I had better bury Al Cullum the teacher and present Al Cullum the person, or else the school year would become monotonous months of trivia. I began to share with my students my moments of joy, my moments of love, my excitement of scholarship, and even my uncertainties. In turn, I discovered the children shared their fears, their strengths, and their hearts with me, and as a professional teacher I responded to their honesty and helped them work out their own opinions and personal values. *Sharing is a key concept* if you are to push back the desks successfully.

Sharing with a class is to capture the spirit of the group and to use this class spirit to step into the unknown. When a teacher can say to his class, "I don't know the answer to that question," then a certain excitement begins to grow within the room as everyone starts to search for the answer.

What is the unknown?

To me, the unknown is initiating a new project in any area of the curriculum. And I truly mean the unknown — not a situation where the teacher has the answer safely tucked away. The unknown is for both students and teachers.

Types of unknowns a teacher can devise are discarding the basal readers and trusting students to read all sorts of books on a subject, using role-playing in social studies instead of the question-answer technique, or allowing students to develop part of the curriculum by listening to their ideas and suggestions for making the presentation of a subject more child-oriented. Other unknowns are reading newspapers instead of language arts workbooks, performing a Shakespearean play, and challenging students to produce their own monthly class newspaper. There are innumerable ways of stepping into the unknown.

In all my projects with children, I stepped into the unknown by doing as much research as they did. For example, in the Parade of Presidents we shared one another's findings about the various presidential administrations without losing respect for one another. We stepped into the unknown together in the rehearsals of every play and dance we produced. Stepping into the unknown together establishes an honest relationship between students and teachers.

There are many teachers throughout the country employing the same methods and techniques I have used, and they are having the same excitement and satisfying results I do. Unfortunately, there are still millions of children who are not developing their own self-starting batteries of success. I'm concerned about all elementary students, particularly those labeled B, C, D, and F students who go through elementary school untouched by any emotion. The A students will probably succeed, but the millions in the middle ranks and the failures who could develop a belief in themselves and make a dream or two come true, those are the ones who need an atmosphere that encourages them to be somebody. By sharing with and joining children in their world, teachers can create an atmosphere for a new kind of learning.

How does a teacher enter the child's world?

Federico Garcia Lorca, the Spanish poet, wrote in "The Ballad of the Little Square":

> I will go very far,
> farther than those hills,
> farther than the seas,
> close to the stars,
> to beg Christ the Lord
> to give back the soul I had
> of old, when I was a child,
> ripened with legends,
> with a feathered cap
> and a wooden sword.

As teachers we should be constantly searching for our lost feathered caps and our lost wooden swords, for they are the only entrees we have to the world of children. If we can't enter their world, we can never reach them. Try donning a feathered cap, wave a wooden sword, and push back your desks!

A Parade of Presidents

"MR. SPEAKER!" "MR. SPEAKER!" resounded from my fifth-grade classroom when a Joint Session of Congress was in full swing!

Other sounds reverberated from this fifth-grade Congress too: the pounding of a gavel calling for order, a roll call being answered by ten-year-old Senators and Congressmen at their respective desks, and whispers from the visitors' gallery, which contained mainly parents. The loudest sound of the morning was the applause as the President of the United States entered the Joint Session of Congress. Senators and Congressmen arose spontaneously as they clapped and showed their respect.

Who was the President of the United States? He was any boy or girl in the class who volunteered to accept the position and was willing to make a State of the Union Address summarizing the accomplishments of his administration. It was a wonderful Parade of Presidents from Washington to Kennedy. Each delivered his message, and each session of Congress supported or questioned him, according to history. From my fifth-grade Parade of Presidents, American history came to life for me for the very first time.

Social studies to me connote live sounds and ideas that are both peaceful and violent; they definitely are not one textbook. One January I became so bored with the social studies text that I collected all the books and stored them away in the cellar of the school. My fifth-graders approved of my actions one hundred per cent and were willing to step into the unknown of American history with me.

In a recent *New York Times Magazine* Arthur M. Schlesinger, Jr., had written an article rating the Presidents of the United States as great, near great, average, below average, and failure. The structure of our Parade of Presidents was based on this essay.

The class very willingly cleared the room of all bulletin board materials and in their places, we hung pictures of the Presidents about the room in chronological order and under each picture posted Mr. Schlesinger's rating.

With this atmosphere of greatness in the room I began a discussion of the role of the President of the United States, the role of a Senator, the role of a Congressman, and the role of the Supreme Court. We discussed the trilogy of power — legislative, executive, and judicial. To give the beginning of the program a sense of freedom, the learning of this subject matter was handled through discussion rather than the method of research. The children asked me many questions until they felt comfortable in having acquired a good idea of how the government of this country works. This discussion lasted about three days, and sometimes I had to do some research to answer their questions.

Then we divided the room into a House of Representatives and a Senate. Some students preferred to be Senators and some were Representatives. Of course minor adjustments were made. Teddy was disappointed when the Senate was overloaded and he had to be a Representative, but there were no serious problems.

To avoid many complications, we decided that it would be best if each child retained the identity of a living Senator or Representative throughout the project. Each Senator and Congressman had his name posted on his desk. Andy was Senator Symington from Missouri, Joanne was Senator Smith of Maine, and Barbara was Representative Adam Clayton Powell of New York. There weren't enough students to include all the living Senators and Representatives, but we had a good sampling.

"Any volunteers to be President of the United States?" Everyone volunteered. In fact, Campbell and Chris were each three different Presidents judiciously spaced in time. We also decided to have a rotating Speaker of the House to give everyone who wanted it the experience of pounding the gavel.

After selecting their presidents, their reading began, for if a child is going to make a State of the Union Address to Congress as President Jefferson, Jackson, or Hoover, a great deal of research work must be done. Further, if a Congressman is to endorse or oppose a President of the United States, a great deal of reading must be done. The students scoured libraries, book stores for paperbacks, attics, and cellars, and they discovered hundreds of books about the Presidents of the United States.

My fifth-graders read and read, and so did I! Each student found his own level of comprehension. They knew what they could understand. The research period lasted approximately one month. Students helped one another! If "Teddy Roosevelt" discovered a book helpful to "Calvin Coolidge," a quick phone call would inform the appropriate student.

The day before President Washington was scheduled to deliver his State of the Union Address, we worked out the following physical arrangement:

1. The classroom was divided in half; the left was the Senate and the right was the House of Representatives.
2. The Speaker of the House's chair faced the class.
3. My large desk served as the podium for the President.
4. The Vice-President's chair was next to the President. I was the Vice-President, and my only function was to keep the facts straight.
5. The visitors' gallery was at the rear of the room. We used wooden platforms and enough folding chairs to accommodate approximately twenty people.
6. The Sergeant at Arms' desk was near the door. His job was to collect visitors' passes and to keep order.

And we posted throughout the community the following schedule:

PRESIDENTIAL SCHEDULE 1962

President George Washington	March 12	Monday
President John Adams	March 13	Tuesday
President Thomas Jefferson	March 15	Thursday
President James Madison	March 16	Friday
President James Monroe	March 19	Monday
President John Quincy Adams	March 20	Tuesday
President Andrew Jackson	March 22	Thursday
President Martin Van Buren	March 23	Friday
President William H. Harrison	March 26	Monday
President John Tyler	March 27	Tuesday
President James K. Polk	March 29	Thursday
President Zachary Taylor	March 30	Friday
President Millard Fillmore	April 2	Monday
President Franklin Pierce	April 3	Tuesday
President James Buchanan	April 5	Thursday
President Abraham Lincoln	April 6	Friday
President Andrew Johnson	April 9	Monday
President Ulysses S. Grant	April 10	Tuesday
President Rutherford B. Hayes	April 12	Thursday
President James A. Garfield	April 13	Friday
President Chester A. Arthur	April 16	Monday
President Grover Cleveland	April 17	Tuesday
President Benjamin Harrison	April 30	Monday
President William McKinley	May 1	Tuesday
President Theodore Roosevelt	May 3	Thursday
President William Howard Taft	May 4	Friday
President Woodrow Wilson	May 7	Monday
President Warren G. Harding	May 8	Tuesday
President Calvin Coolidge	May 10	Thursday
President Herbert Hoover	May 21	Monday
President Franklin D. Roosevelt	May 22	Tuesday
President Harry S. Truman	May 23	Wednesday
President Dwight D. Eisenhower	May 24	Thursday
President John F. Kennedy	May 25	Friday

There was a bit of trouble at the railroad station because some of the children had placed the circulars on commuters' car windshields, but no one was arrested.

There was great excitement when the Parade of Presidents commenced. The visitors' gallery was jammed with people who were curious to see what President Washington would have to say. David, the Speaker of the House, completed the roll call; everyone was present. Wayne, the Sergeant at Arms announced, "Ladies and Gentlemen, the President of the United States!"

Soon the visitors realized that this was not a bit of nonsense but a touch of greatness in the social studies program, a touch of greatness that made American history come alive. It was exciting to hear President Washington discuss the Whiskey Rebellion in Pennsylvania and how he handled the situation in a skillful manner; it was exciting to hear him present his new plans for a brand-new Capitol and to learn that it would be located on the eastern bank of the Potomac River; it was exciting listening to him advise Congress that America should remain neutral when dealing with European powers.

"War for an unarmed, new country such as ours would be disastrous!" said President Washington.

"Mr. President, are you very upset that Vice-President Adams called you a muttonhead?" asked a Senator.

The Representative from California rose and said, "Mr. Speaker, I vote that we give President Washington a unanimous vote of confidence for the work he has been doing to keep such a young country unified."

Just before he left, the President informed the Joint Session of Congress that he was planning to make a tour

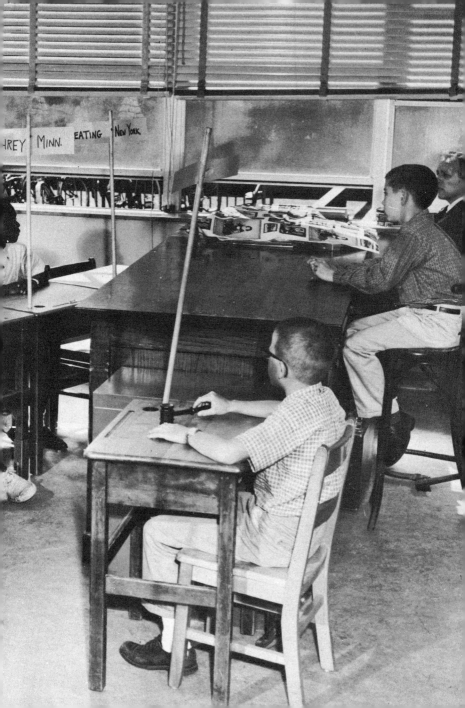

of the country to see firsthand the needs of the people. President Washington received thunderous applause as he left the room. I signaled the Sergeant at Arms to close the door quickly so other classes would not be disturbed.

The class then agreed with Mr. Schlesinger that President Washington should be rated a great President. The children didn't always agree with Mr. Schlesinger though, particularly in the case of President Grant. They couldn't bring themselves to vote him a failure for two reasons: (1) even though he had not been a good President, how could people forget his great contributions in the Civil War, and (2) how could anyone be branded a failure?

President Washington had been nervous just before he entered Congress, but any normal fifth-grader would be nervous. Even the real President must be slightly nervous as he prepares to address the real Congress. I don't believe the real President Johnson has to go to the bathroom three times before he enters Congress as my President Washington did, but after an hour's discussion with Congress, my President Washington left the session with a feeling of greatness and a feeling of success that will remain with him always!

All the Presidents were touched by the greatness of their office. They carried themselves with dignity; they exuded a confidence of leadership; they spoke with much belief. Of course some were better than others, but they all succeeded. I was always there as Vice-President to help or to encourage if necessary. Isn't that our job as teachers — to help? What greater gift can we give our students than a lasting feeling of success?

It was amazing how each student captured the personality of the President he represented. For example, Margie, as President John Quincy Adams, gave us a half-hour of John Quincy Adams temperament. It was very moving when Peter, as President Wilson, pleaded with Congress to approve his Fourteen Points, when Cathy, as President Grant, admitted "he" was a better General than President and that "he" also drank a great deal, and when President Hoover reminded Congress that the Depression was not all his fault.

Even more exciting was when the members of Congress would not vote according to history. There were moments when they refused to vote for levying income taxes and refused to declare war when history said war had been declared. Perhaps most exciting of all was when my fifth-graders were ahead of the times, as when they were ready to give women the right to vote years before history did. This is where the Vice-President stepped in and reminded them that it was necessary to stick to the facts, whether they agreed or not.

What a learning situation — not a teaching situation but a learning situation!

As March, April, and May rolled by and each President presented his successes and problems, many surprises unfolded. What a surprise to all what a prominent part President James Polk played in the growth of our country, what a surprise how little some Presidents accomplished, what a surprise to discover the role the President played throughout the world, what a surprise to recognize the narrow-mindedness of the public. . . . one surprise after another.

From that one small classroom came the sounds of America — sounds based on facts discovered by each individual student, facts I didn't know, facts they wanted to know. But more important than the facts was the fervid exploration of books that even Ponce de Leon's search for the Fountain of Youth could not equal!

My fifth-grade Congressmen read all types of books, for they felt a sense of responsibility to know what they were talking about. They wanted their opinions to be based on facts when they discussed the balance of power in the United States, the Republican and Democratic Parties, the repealing of Amendments, the problems of labor, or the problems of a depression. These words meant something now. They were not just words at the end of a chapter or words on a teacher's quiz.

Through reading the students learned the responsibilities involved in being a President, the satisfaction of helping one's country, and the common problems of Presidents. They read about Congress, the threats and pressures of the public, the physical growth of the country, and the fights to become President. They also injected into their learning their hopes for future Presidents of the United States. They hoped that future Presidents would unite all nations into one big family and abolish the upper and lower classes. They hoped it would be possible to have a Negro President, a Jewish President, and a woman President. They had many hopes!

What were they reading? They were reading much more than a basic social studies text could possibly offer. They went from encyclopedias to the latest, hot-off-the-press paperback books. Sometimes they went way over their heads in their reading, but I was there to give them a helping hand.

The children read with a comprehension that was astounding! Why? They read because they were excited! Reading with the objective of comprehending, students found it difficult to understand why Congress did not support President Wilson's ideas, and they understood how silly Prohibition was when one young Congressman stated that there was no law in the world that could stop her father from drinking! Silent and comprehensive reading made them realize how the United States was originally able to stay out of foreign entanglements but as the nation developed and as transportation improved, they began to sense what an influence it was in foreign affairs. They saw a little nation go through adolescent problems, specifically the Civil War. They read about a nation being so well balanced that a weak President could not destroy its structure. They read, they understood, and my students conquered!

What about vocabulary development? The children used many new words, words such as veto, impeachment, representative, diplomatic relations, tariff, administration, compromise, debates, slavery, and alliance and they knew what they meant. Senators were asking other Senators to defend his or her own point of view concerning such words. You cannot defend a high tariff if you do not fully understand what a tariff is.

What about writing? A newspaper was published daily. It announced that a specific President was speaking that particular day or the next day, and it consisted of student-gathered material. A team of students distributed the paper throughout the city. Each student was responsible for furnishing the news for at least one issue, and many did more than one.

At the very end of the project, the students wrote a book about the Presidents of the United States. First of all they decided that the book should be called *MR. SPEAKER!* for those were the two most used words in the Parade of Presidents project.

"President McKinley's" mother assisted as our short-hand expert. The children blurted out various areas and topics they thought would make good chapters, and Mrs. Wright wrote them down as fast as she could. I used the technique of having a shorthand expert so that the children would retain their spontaneity and the group dynamics process would not be slowed down by having the students do the writing at this stage of creating. Thoughtful writing by the students would come later. The next day each student received a dittoed copy of approximately forty ideas, and the class decided which ones should be written up for the book. Some of the chapters the children chose were "The Triangle of Power," "The Responsibility of Being President," "Congress and the Presidency," "The Public and Amendments," "Future Presidents," and many others.

At this point students volunteered to write the chapters, and as a group we decided that it would be best and more fun to work in pairs. It took about two months to work the chapters into good shape; many revisions and much proofreading were required. This project served as a good language arts-social studies combination. The facts had to be correct and clear to the reader. Six students did the art work, and we were ready for publication. Then a problem arose — we had no money! Dr. Joseph Grimes, Jr., then Superintendent of Schools, came to the rescue. He provided us with a secretary who neatly typed our chapters, and he found some money some place in the budget for stencils, paper, binders, and the reproduction of our cover. With student volunteer help during the summer, the book was finally put together, and as a climax the authors invited the community to a book lawn party. Each student received two copies of the book — one for his home and one perhaps for grandparents.

Sometimes there would be one person, sometimes twenty, in the visitors' gallery, but the children ignored the gallery and threw themselves into American history. Teachers who say observers disturb their classes and distract their students are correct — but only if they have uninvolved students! Pupils who are in the midst of a creative situation are oblivious to visitors.

The children all became thoroughly involved with the exciting growth of their nation and learned from the project the mistakes of past generations. They questioned the handling of the Indians; they praised President Monroe and his Monroe Doctrine; they felt President Polk should receive more credit; they thought it a shame that some men became Presidents by accident rather than merit; they wondered if Teddy Roosevelt was a bully or an inspirational leader. Some agreed with the President that a high tariff was necessary; some disagreed violently and gave valid reasons. They felt great sympathy for President Andrew Johnson having to follow the greatness of President Lincoln and were reluctant to even mention impeachment proceedings.

All this convinced me that such a social studies project has a place in all levels of the elementary school curriculum, year in and year out. For instance, primary children can pretend to be famous explorers, Indians, or early colonists and through re-enacting events of the past will develop an understanding of and love for American history.

I truly believe such a program *is* education and a vital part of the curriculum. There were no tests or quizzes or failures. Of course some students were better Presidents than others, but the important objective was to acquire a taste of American history, not an A, B$^+$, or an F. Congress quite often helped a President who was slightly floundering, and as Vice-President I helped out. No one failed!

How did I evaluate my students when the time came to place a social studies mark on their report cards? I gave them all A's, because there was not one emotionally dishonest President in the whole class.

The Parade of Presidents was a classroom success . . . earned success! Being a President of the United States constituted a step forward in developing belief in themselves, something the family alone cannot furnish. Students must earn success through the structure of the school, and the school must find the success level of each child.

Yes, there were many sounds emanating from that fifth-grade Joint Session of Congress. The sound of the rights of women, the sound of violence that finally erupted into World War II, the sound of disagreement over Prohibition, the sound of a broken heart when Congress voted against the League of Nations, the sound of a Presidential veto! Endless sounds and feelings. No matter where those particular fifth-graders venture, they will carry with them always a piece of American history, for they were part of the Parade of Presidents!

By re-enacting Congress, the intricacies of our government and its history were made simple by discussions among ourselves. I can remember many of the debates we had in class, and these helped me to be a better participator, which now accounts for one-third of a semester grade in many of my high school classes. I learned to be an independent thinker, a "builder-upper" rather than a "tearer-downer," a sportsman, and a connoisseur of the arts.

Campbell Gerrish, 1962

I remember our Congress so clearly that it might have happened yesterday. I have often looked through Mr. Speaker! *the book the class wrote, and I still haven't lost interest.*

Peter Brophy, 1962

The Class 5A Congress was a great project in that every student could and did contribute something to the class. Each student could work at his own level. The result was that everyone was stimulated by a challenge proportional to the work they could handle. Added to this, there was constant excitement in the classroom because we were impersonating great men. I don't doubt that at times I thought I was the man I was impersonating, which led to great ideas.

Jim Pugh, 1962

As you might remember, history was not my best subject, but you took the dullness out of it and thereby made it entertaining and exciting.

Gail Henefield, 1962

Perhaps the most distinct of all the adventures in the fifth-grade was the Congress. I portrayed President Adams, President Polk, and Lincoln. I think I learned more American history from this project than any other course I have ever taken.

Chris Ley, 1962

In the Parade of Presidents I felt I was playing my own part in history. I learned and at the same time enjoyed it. History seemed to come alive.

Joanne Wible, 1962

The most exciting project was the Congress. I remember laboring over magazines and newspapers, trying to keep up with what President Kennedy did. I remember the excitement of taking the oath of office, of a packed gallery, of having arguments with the members of Congress. It was a challenging, exciting experience — one which I shall never forget.

Barbara Zelner, 1962

Elementary School Pulitzers

MANY TIMES AS A beginning teacher I used to say to my classes:

"I insist that you write complete sentences!"

"All I want is complete, concise thoughts!"

"Can't you be more original?"

"How can you possibly forget to put in the period!"

"Ever hear of using a dictionary?"

"Almost every other word is misspelled!"

"This composition is too short!"

"This composition is too long!"

"Be more creative!"

One day I heard the echoes of my admonitions, and in an embarrassed fashion I asked myself, "What have you written lately?"

How difficult it is for most adults to write; even penning a little thank-you note brings out beads of sweat. With all the rules established by non-writing teachers, it's no wonder that the most painful job of the elementary school child is to pick up his pencil and write. Write what? All the teacher's rules are bad enough, but write what???

To write *honestly* is to expose oneself, and how many nine-, ten-, eleven-, or twelve-year-olds are willing to expose themselves to teachers with all their rules of right and wrong? With a limited vocabulary, lack of trust in the person at the front of the room, and years of writing such foolishness as

> The leaves are falling
> And mother is calling!

it's no wonder fourth-, fifth-, and sixth-graders write poorly. They may write neatly and quietly, but their writing is dull as dishwater. Children write safely. They are usually reluctant to let teachers enter their world, which, according to all the child psychology books, is a fantastic, creative, spontaneous world. Maybe we have too many rules; maybe students want us to share our world — our creative world — with them. Why should they be the only ones to expose themselves?

One September very early in the school year, in fact the second day, I announced to my sixth-graders that there would be a great deal of writing throughout the year. The more adventuresome students groaned and moaned. They glanced sadly at one another — the year was going to be a nightmare.

I continued to explain that all writing would be on a voluntary basis. All smiles! It was like Christmas Eve and the last day of school rolled into one! It was like the peak of the Fourth of July when I announced:

"No book reports this year!"

"No reading workbooks this year!"

"No original weekly poems!"

"In place of all this, I'm going to explore your minds as you explore mine. Every once in a while I will assign a phrase, and if you can't think of anything to write about it, that's O.K. I will attempt to express *my thoughts in writing* also."

A dead branch . . . a box of chocolates . . . a quiet room. . . . These were just a few of the subjects we all wrote about, sometimes for only five minutes, sometimes during a weekend. Of course it was not very creative of me to impose my topics upon the children, but it was the beginning of their believing in what they were writing. They saw that I was expressing myself in writing right along with them and that I was not passing judgment on their honest emotions. They began to trust me.

At first it was difficult for many to write. In fact one girl had a temper tantrum in the middle of her living room floor carpet on a Sunday evening when she screamed at her mother, "He wants me to think . . . and I can't think! He wants me to be honest . . . and I can't be . . . honest!"

She could think and she could be honest, and a few weeks later she was writing with much less difficulty. She was slowly discarding the role of the student and becoming herself. She was beginning to realize that she had many things to say, besides the things expected of her.

One December morning an unexpected incident occurred that helped us tremendously to become more spontaneous in our approach to writing. A forlorn-looking alley cat had jumped up on the ledge outside our window, and, of course, the class responded to the cat's meowing by saying, practically in unison, "Let her in, Mr. Cullum."

One stern, strict rule of this particular school was that no live animals were allowed, but we let her in anyway. I requested the class to remain absolutely silent and not to touch the cat but simply to watch her. For about twenty minutes we observed, fascinated by our roaming cat.

I then suggested that they not only observe but quickly write impressions about our visitor, moods created by her presence, or personal thoughts about the cat. Here are some examples of the writing done that morning.

It was a gray misty morning,
I was expecting something dull,
Instead we had something quite a
    bit different,
A brown-sugar-colored kitty cat!
The whole business was quite secret,
This most extraordinary thing.
Now, outside of the school
There was a little dog
That kept barking at a kitty cat,
So in a very secret manner
We gave the cat a home,
Not in the school yard,
But in our very own room!
                            Joan Emery

We have a mysterious visitor,
He comes from the wind and the cold.
He might have a little bitty sore
From the dog out in the wind and the cold!
It's a cat, a lonely frightened cat,
It looks for warmth and care.

He looks for a nice clean bed,
He's gentle and never gets in our hair.

Ted Haley

I walked into the room,
Not one person did stir.
I could not see a thing,
But I heard a little purr.

I looked around the place,
Nothing did I see.
But then I saw a cat
Sitting near Pete's knee.

It gave to me the feeling
That this cat was a queen
For everyone was kind to her,
As kind as you've ever seen.

Everyone was quiet
So this poor cat could sleep.
He had been in a fight
With a dog from the deep.

Joanne Wible

When the majority of my fifth- and sixth-graders were comfortable in the knowledge that I was not going to slash their works to bits, I introduced them to the name Joseph Pulitzer, the poor, uneducated immigrant who became one of the greatest American newspaper publishers and left two million dollars to Columbia University as an endowment for prizes for the advancement of education. Each year a Pulitzer Prize is awarded in the fields of journalism, literature, music, and art. Then I began to explain my Elementary School Pulitzer Prize plan:

"Here it is October 15th. You have until May first to

to work for an Elementary School Pulitzer Prize in the field of the novel, short story, poetry, essay, or play. I will be here to help you and guide you, but only if you so desire. It is not easy to work all year on a project and be critical of your own work, but those who want to try for an Elementary School Pulitzer Prize will have my wholehearted support at any time of the day. You may call me at home or interrupt me at will, for I will be there to offer advice if you want it. Those who do not want to attempt such a project — we still love you. Of course, the Elementary School Pulitzer Prize Winners' works will be published!"

Almost everyone was eager to participate, and as the days, weeks, and months rolled by, slowly but surely the children submitted their efforts for my evaluation and advice. I was very careful not to impose my creative standards, or substandards, upon their work. I made such comments as:

"Don't worry about your spelling; just write what you think."

"I don't care how short your poems are."

"Of course poems don't have to rhyme."

"If you want to be critical of your family and your school, go right ahead as long as you believe in what you're saying."

"When you run out of thoughts, don't write! More thoughts will come later."

"Relax!"

"It's nicely written, but I don't believe you!"

"If you love your dog, write about the love you have for him."

"If you hate your brother, write about hating him."

There were no grades, no deletion marks, no red pencil checks, and certainly no remarks about handwriting — there was just an exchange of comments.

Sometimes the children wrote in school, but most of the time they wrote at home. One young student kept a pad and pencil near her bed to be able to scribble her thoughts as she was falling asleep. Some of the most profound thoughts occur as you fall into a light sleep, she told me.

Another young lady decided to postpone writing her three-act play and concentrated on a one-act play. In her case this was a sensible compromise. Some students had conferences with me to discuss their discouragement, and I always reminded them that this was not an assignment. If it was no longer an interesting experience for them, I advised them to put the project aside for about a month. Perhaps they could try again later.

There were some problems with parents who wanted to help their children, but as the children gained in confidence they resisted parental assistance.

By the time May rolled around some, of course, had thrown in the sponge, and I assured them that it was all right. After all, they were only ten- and eleven-year-olds, and it wasn't necessary to write the great American novel right then and there.

On May first I was nervous during the day as students submitted their collections of poems, their novels, their essays, and their short stories — and one three-act play appeared upon the desk. I was disappointed that certain students hadn't extended themselves and happily surprised and startled that others had.

I pored through the manuscripts that night, disillusioned at times, exhilarated at others. I experienced a warm feeling when certain students exposed their souls in their creative efforts. They had something to say and said it!

ANNOUNCEMENTS FROM THE OFFICE OF THE PRINCIPAL

Monday Morning:	The Pulitzer Prize Winner for the novel is Martha Birnbaum.
Tuesday Morning:	The Pulitzer Prize Winners for poetry are: Carmela De-Carlo, Jonathan Lawson, Chris Ley, Sloan MacDonald, Donald O'Dell, and Mary True.
Wednesday Morning:	The Pulitzer Prize Drama Award goes to Susan Walker.
Thursday Morning:	The Pulitzer Prize Essay Winner is — none.
Friday Morning:	The Pulitzer Prize Short Story Award is shared by Nancy Baker, Joan Emery, and James Jaffray.

There was great excitement that week for Joseph Pulitzer had provided our public school with a touch of greatness. As promised, the Pulitzer Prize Winners' works were published. Unfortunately I had not planned for the project in my budget, and there was not a nickel at my disposal. How could I have planned for this in June when the idea didn't strike me until September? Anyway, a New York City printer sympathized with my plight and lowered his price, and each Pulitzer Prize Winner received a paperback booklet of his work.

The years have gone by, but I still glance through the volume entitled *The Midland School Pulitzer Price Win-*

ners, Spring 1963, and I reread the short story by Joan Emery, sixth-grader:

Next to Heaven

Running, running, running with my mouth open so the wild air could fill my lungs. The sand tickles our feet and scratches our toes. Running till we dropped with exhaustion. Teasing the waves by never letting them quite reach us. This is the life one leads on the end of Nantucket, the place next to heaven.

SHIP AHOY! We were in the middle of playing shipwreck, pretending to be abandoned in the dunes of Nantucket. Shells were plates, and boards tables. The dunes were separated in places, creating natural rooms. I and my friends and my dog played in the place next to heaven. Paddling, paddling, paddling through streams that only by a fallboat were navigable, we felt the thrill of exploring places that few others had explored before. Feeling alone and independent in the place next to heaven.

Then slowly things began to happen. Things were beginning to be packed, and the next thing I knew we were getting into our car, preparing to leave, and my friends came out and chased our car as long as they could. I faced with much difficulty the fact that we were leaving the place next to heaven. Smoke filled my lungs and took the place of fresh air. Shoes enclosed my once free, sand-covered feet. Sorrow filled my heart, taking the place of freedom and joy.

Never again will I go to the place next to heaven.

I never fail to reread Chris Ley's poetry:

The Middle Ages

The clash, the clank, the cling,
As the swords in Make Believe ring.
The child pretending he's someone

Who could slay anyone he'd ever laid eyes on.
This fighter so brave, stabbing his shadow,
While wrecking the house and eating an apple
Was being threatened by one big danger.
His one rival, the first he'd laid eyes on
In the castle through the hall,
Then through the living room
Lived this only rival,
The castle made up of the kitchen.
This castle guarded by this one rival,
And it made the boy tremble,
THE MOTHER!

She would threaten him,
Maybe she would throw him in the dungeon.
The dungeon was ordinary,
Deep, dark, and all the comforts of home.
When she saw the mess
He had made,
He could guess what she would say!
"You bad little boy,
I'll spank you!"

The boy shuddered and thought,
I'll be six soon
And out of the Middle Childhood,
I'll be called a big boy,
No more five-year-old games,
And no more Middle Ages!

That is a beautiful, sensitive poem by an eleven-year-old. Among his collection is another I always enjoy reading:

In and Out

Out goes big brother for school,
As little brother watches.
The door slams

As little brother goes into the kitchen.
This is the daily morning,
And these are the daily questions.
Where is big brother going?
When will he be back?
When can I go with him?
What is school?

After a year of this he changes his routine.
Now *he* wanted to go to school.
He had a reason to ask questions.
He had a teacher to answer them now.
His relieved mother sighed, pushed him out the door.
This was so he wouldn't ask another question.

After his joyful graduation of kindergarten
He was ready to ask more questions.
In and out he ran asking more questions,
And it came that joyful day!
But what was this?
He didn't want to go back!

This isn't unusual,
It had to happen.
So, it's in your mind one year
And out the next.

Here is one more Chris Ley poem, for he is my favorite
elementary school poet:

Strange Medical Care

The boys went off
To play army again,
Running in and out of the brush ˎ
And being careful they are not shot.
They brought along the best doctor
And bet he could cure anyone.
No one was hurt yet,
But we spoke too soon.

They had just found the enemy,
And someone got wounded.

"Quickly Doc, he's hurt!"

The Doc went over and pretended to do something,
Then he kissed the wound.
They asked him what that would do.
"It will cure the pain," he said.
"My Mom does it to me
And it never fails."

This medical care was new,
But they accepted it.

When elementary school children are confident enough to expose their thoughts through creative expression, the results are marvelous. Their creativity has a frail strength that adults can never emulate. Creative writing by elementary school children is poetry in action. When they share with you, feel most honored!

Your creative writing class was a great help. Although we were only eleven, I feel we developed a sense of originality and perceptiveness. It was a way to freely express oneself. Looking back on those years, I can see how really worthwhile and fun they were.
Susan Hadley, 1960

The first thing I felt really involved in was the Pulitzer Prize Winners of which I was one of the winners with my poems. The thing is that the satisfaction for me came mostly from the fact that I was actually doing some work. *Still, every once in a while, I write a poem or two, remembering that satisfaction.*

Mary True, 1963

The Language Enrichment Class was a chance to express myself without the rules of structure and punctuation or the pressure of grades tying me down. What I put down on paper was the real me, not just a mass of words thrown together to please the teacher. I think the basic achievement of this class was that it taught each of us to look for the feelings inside ourself and to express them in any way we could. And the language bulletins helped as incentive because there is nothing more rewarding than seeing your own words in print.

Merrily Gerrish, 1960

The Renoir Room

WE TURNED OUR sixth-grade classroom into a Renoir Room! How exciting it was to step into the unknown world of this great French painter.

After emptying the room of all vestiges of school life — textbooks, bulletin boards, announcements, school menus, and the wastepaper basket — the magic began. Slowly but delightedly the students hung the first Renoir painting, and then the next, and the next, until fifty-four reproductions of Renoir paintings were displayed on the four classroom walls. Some were small, some large, some first-rate Renoirs, others not so good, but a magic was there, a greatness was there, and that's all that mattered for the moment.

The desks were out in the hallway, and the chairs were arranged for a public school art gallery, that is, they were placed in small groups of threes and fours facing clusters of Renoirs.

Now we had a Renoir Room with no textbooks and no desks. No learning? Wrong! We had created the type of learning situation that really counts — a type of learning situation that helps a student to grow and at the same time proves to him the value of his skills and of learning to read.

The purpose of this project was to have students enter the world of Renoir through the beauty of his work, to engage in independent research to discover the man Renoir, and to digest and share this newly found world with the rest of the school.

The students ventured into the world of Renoir through intensive reading and research in the school library, the public library, and books at home and in the local bookstore, The Lighthouse. They pored over art books, biographies, and references. At one point the public librarian complained that too many students from my class were in the library and that it didn't have that many books about Renoir.

A whole new world of words opened up to them — impression, spontaneity, inspiration, technique, contemporary, classical, realism, modern, creative freedom, palette, influence, neo-impressionist, opaque, original, vigor, sensibility, dynamic, master, exquisite, salon, composition, texture, bourgeois, progressive, austerity, chromatic, post-impressionism, and many, many more. What a wonderful new wealth of words the students learned, used, and understood.

The fifty-four Renoir paintings became more meaningful as each day progressed. The life of Renoir became alive. His rich, creative life became known to the entire class because, to be thoroughly prepared to talk about

Renoir, students had to read more than the school's encyclopedia. That's why students come to school — not to learn how to read, but to read, to explore new worlds through reading, to digest challenging material, and to gain pleasure and enjoyment.

Once all the data had been accumulated by individual note-taking (no notes were scrutinized by me), the class had to determine what facts to use for the lectures they intended to give. The children had to decide how best to hold the attention of the various groups to whom they would talk about Renoir. What would be interesting for a sixth-grade class might not be of interest to a first-grade group, and then there was the problem of how to approach adult groups who were coming after school. As it turned out, not too many adults attended, for they did not fully grasp the importance of their roles in this lecture series.

It is not an easy matter to decide how to adjust a lecture to various age levels. As teachers we must give students every opportunity to organize and decide on their own. The classroom teacher sets up the structure — in this case the Renoir Room — but the students must make all the decisions. They decided with whom they would work, they decided what phase of Renoir's art they would emphasize, they decided to what age-level group they would like to lecture, and they decided if they wanted to volunteer to participate in the project.

The day arrived when Ann and Louise were ready to give the first lecture to a third-grade group. It was Miss Hall's class, and her youngsters were quite excited as they entered a classroom that was an art gallery — a new world for them. Good schools introduce students to as many new worlds as possible.

The third-graders were initially startled by the fifty-four paintings. After they were seated the lecture began. The two girls were nervous at first because they were not quite sure if they could capture the interest of these eight-year-olds. Soon, however, they perceived a quiet attentiveness in the room as the lecture progressed, and then they knew that those twenty-four third-graders were with them.

Louise left the makeshift rostrum and, with a pointer in hand, circulated about the gallery pointing out various masterpieces such as "Two Girls at the Piano," "Madame Charpentier and Her Daughters," "Luncheon of the Boating Party," "The Swing," "The Bridge," and so forth. As she was talking, Louise sensed which paintings were favored by the group and which paintings did not impress them. After she finished her tour, Ann completed the lecture with some final comments about their being such respectful guests and reminded them to be sure to circulate about the Renoir Room and make any comment they chose to. Also, cookies would be served! The idea of cookies pleased everyone, and it was most interesting to observe the youngsters nibbling cookies and commenting about the art work:

"His women are fat!"

"I like his clouds."

"I don't like any of them."

"He's my favorite painter now."

"I like the boy writing the best."

"How much do they cost?"

"That woman is wearing a funny hat."

Then it was time for Miss Hall's children to return to their classroom. They thanked the two lecturers and filed out. That afternoon after school five third-graders returned to visit the Renoir Room — and only one asked for a cookie.

The Renoir Room lasted for two weeks during which many lectures were presented to all age groups. Every lecture was a success. The idea spread. The Midland School librarian allowed us to set up in her library a Picasso Palace that consisted of fifty Picasso paintings representing his five periods. At Osborn School the librarian began a program of lending reproductions for a week.

Children were being exposed to greatness, and they were responding positively.

Did every class visit the Renoir Room? Of course not! Why? It was not in the curriculum, and besides, how could a second-grader possibly understand Renoir? My answer was quite simple — "They would understand Renoir as a second-grader could understand Renoir." I reminded the skeptics how, in response to a question about the meaning of his abstract works, Picasso once replied to the effect, "How does one explain the song of a bird? I paint for all ages, not just twenty-seven-year-olds."

Out of the Renoir Room came a love of a particular painting entitled "The Skiff." Jimmy loved this painting so much that he requested that it be one of his Christmas presents, and I believe it is now hanging in the family living room. Also out of that Renoir Room came reading that would make the reading workbooks blush . . . dictionary work that made sense and was practical . . .

speeches and recitations that had a purpose and were not just parrot work. Writing took place . . . writing ads to publicize the Renoir Room . . . writing opinions of the work of Renoir. The students fed on Renoir — they feasted on this touch of greatness!

What does turning a classroom into a Renoir Room or a Cezanne Cellar have to do with school work? As one father so aptly expressed it, "I want my kid to go to school to learn . . . yeah, even Renoir and all that crap!"

My phrasing is not quite that direct. I simply want children to be exposed to as many things as possible in all elementary grades. Sometimes at this level a tremendous impact occurs between student and greatness! Greatness can exist every day in each classroom — not only in the room of the specialists, but in every everyday classroom with every everyday teacher.

If a teacher doesn't like the soft pastel world of Renoir, then why not turn the classroom into a Chagall Chamber, or a Degas Den, or a Modigliani Mansion? But do turn your classroom into something and at least once a year expose your students to an unknown quantity. Step back and let the students explore. Step way back, and let the experience be their success, not something you taught them. When children achieve success on their own, a love of the subject develops and they have an exhilarating sense of fulfillment that never fades away.

Prints needed for a classroom gallery are not expensive. Don't wait for petty cash or school board approval, or your gallery will never open. Prints can be purchased in almost any book store for about $2 each, or they can be borrowed from most local public libraries. Obtain the cardboard prints for they are more receptive to rougher handling.

Why wait until students go to the art teacher to be exposed to a great painting? The same is true with music. Why wait till the music period? When children enter an everyday classroom in the morning, why shouldn't Toscanini be conducting?

If the excitement of greatness does not exist in your own school, create your own room of greatness. Of course you can't do it all by yourself, but you can obtain all the help you need from the painters of the world and the composers and the writers. Children grasp greatness very quickly!

Through the art projects in class, I gained a knowledge of various art works and techniques. I also was inspired to create my own opinions and interpretations of the paintings. I have never since had the opportunity to absorb so much information about art in a classroom.

Sherry Hensley, 1963

I still have the painting "The Tragedy" by Picasso.

Gary Gilch, 1961

I first saw Da Vinci's "Mona Lisa" in your classroom and learned the complexities of her smile. The other various paintings you put up I still keep coming across and probably always will.

Jim Hadley, 1961

Frequently people will ask what was my most enlightening school year. When I answer "fifth-grade," people sometimes appear surprised, but in my case fifth-grade was the most challenging and rewarding year. To this day I often find myself browsing through art books or walking through museums, happy that I can recognize certain artists, while my mind is being flooded with fifth-grade memories.

Teddy Martin, 1960

I also found the identification of famous paintings very interesting. I still remember some of the famous scenes and their artists.

Bill Cornelius, 1959

I still have the painting "Portrait of a Girl" by Modigliani in my room.

Ira Shuman, 1960

Kindergarten Chatter

FROM MY MEAGER LINEN CLOSET I sacrificed a good white sheet to make a dramatic entrance into the Milton School kindergarten in Rye, New York. As a roaming language arts teacher I was able to indulge in such activity, and when a homeroom teacher such as Mrs. Lipman gave me the opportunity to experiment, I took advantage of the situation.

There I was in the middle of the kindergarten covered with my last good sheet, in which two holes had been cut out for my eyes. I saw twenty-two pairs of eyes looking at me.

"I am a friendly apparition," I slowly stated.

"What's that?" asked five-year-old Tony.

"Talk to me and find out!"

They all started to talk at once, of course, so I asked them to sit in a circle, and I sat in the center. I proceeded to whirl about in a flashing dervish manner and explained to them that for Halloween I was going to be a very friendly apparition.

"What do I look like?"

Finally Annette guessed that I was dressed as a ghost. They then took turns wearing the large sheet and practically flew through the kindergarten air as friendly apparitions. It was very simple for them to accept "apparition" as a good kindergarten word.

The next day we gathered again in our magic circle, and again I was an apparition, but this time I was also shaking a box with something inside that made a jingling-jangling sound.

"What's inside my box?" I asked.

The answers ranged from candy, money, stones, and pennies to teeth.

"Yes, I have pennies, nickels, dimes, and quarters in my box. But altogether what are they called?"

They couldn't guess, and finally I told them the word — "coins." Each child in the magic circle had a chance to shake the coins. Later that morning we practiced a little speech. Someone would go out in the hallway and knock on the door.

"Come in," we all yelled!

Billy entered and said, "Trick or Treat. I am collecting for UNICEF. Do you have any coins to contribute to UNICEF?"

Everyone again had a chance to jangle the coins in the box.

The day before Halloween the magic circle turned into a circle of pumpkins. I asked each pumpkin to make a face. I touched Francine on the head and said, "What a happy countenance your pumpkin has."

To David I remarked, "What an angry countenance your pumpkin has, and yours, too, Sarah."

To Anita I said, "What a comical countenance your pumpkin has."

Soon it dawned upon the magic circle of pumpkins that countenance meant face, and then and there we practiced the rest of the morning making various countenances. We felt each other's faces with closed eyes to see if we could identify correctly the expression of the countenance. From this experience of feeling countenances stemmed the words "nostrils," "ear lobes," "clavicle," "cranium," and even "saliva" — one countenance had an open mouth!

One day sitting in the center of the magic circle I pounded two ash can covers together. "Crash! Bang! Crash! Smash!" How they loved the noise. Some covered their ears but didn't want me to stop.

"Why do some of you cover your ears?"

"The noise was too loud," said Elizabeth.

"My ears hurt," replied Steve.

"Was it a big noise?"

"YES!" they all yelled.

"Was I making a clamor?"

"YES!" they all yelled.

And of course, all that week whenever someone was making too much noise, the kindergarten children would say, "Stop the clamor!"

The next week I gathered the circle together and started bawling and crying like a baby.

"Stop the clamor!" they cried.

"You have to call me by my right name before I do!"

They finally guessed that I was a baby who was hungry. Then I introduced the word "infant." They took turns in the middle of the circle imitating an infant. Naturally they imitated their baby brothers and sisters whom some liked and others disliked.

One day I read to the children the poem "Fog" by Carl Sandburg and at the end I said, "Now you sit on your haunches."

They couldn't fathom the word haunches, but as soon as I asked them to sit as a cat would sit, the magic circle of twenty-two became twenty-two cats sitting on their haunches. We all found it very comfortable sitting on our haunches.

Another time I flapped and flapped my arms, sometimes slowly and calmly and other times frantically. They guessed correctly when they said I was a bird.

"But what about my arms that are always moving, sometimes slowly and sometimes swiftly? What are they called besides wings?"

Naturally they couldn't guess the word "pinions," but they accepted the word without batting an eyelash. Everyone used his pinions that day.

One bright sunny morning I stood in the middle of the kindergarten room with my face looking directly into the fluorescent light. I started crowing like a rooster. They guessed immediately that I was a big rooster, and they too indulged in some barnyard antics.

"Now I'm going to be a special rooster . . . a very proud bright red rooster." Right then and there, with full lung power, I burst forth into a crowing never heard before in the elementary school world. They were impressed. Slowly but surely we sounded out the word "chanticleer." They seemed to crow even better now that they were chanticleers.

Another day I played for them some merry-go-round music on the piano. The magic circle started slowly to move as a merry-go-round. Faster went my hands and faster went the magic circle merry-go-round. Abruptly I stopped the music. "What's another word for merry-go-round?"

One child knew. It was Susan. "Carrousel."

The magic circle carrousel moved round and round, and up and down. It was a delightful merry-go-round . . . excuse me, carrousel.

One day the magic circle gathered, and I pranced and snorted and cavorted.

"Horse!" they all yelled.

"Almost!"

"Wild horse," bellowed Timothy.

"Almost."

Finally I told them I was a stallion.

"What's a stallion?" inquired Meg.

I did not give them the dictionary definition that a stallion is an uncastrated male horse but simply told them that I was a big horse and very proud.

"Now get ready, boys and girls, for I'm going to try to jump over the magic circle fence!"

They braced themselves determined that I wouldn't be able to get out — and I didn't. I couldn't break through those firmly clenched hands.

The best day was when I was a huge wave and they were sandpipers pecking for food on the beach. They screamed and squealed as they avoided the splash of the big wave as they raced to safety by touching the black-board.

It was exciting to see them go home during the school year as twenty-two eerie apparitions, twenty-two well-trained pachyderms, twenty-two proud, snorting stallions, and twenty-one (one absent) crowing chanticleers. They carried their big words home to astounded parents, grandparents, and older brothers and sisters. They were proud of their new words. Together we had added sixty new words to their speaking vocabulary.

At the end of the year I devised a test to see how well they had retained their big words. Without any review, over 90 per cent of the class scored one hundred! The words were still alive!

During the year they called me Mr. Question, never Mr. Cullum, for as Beth said, "You always ask so many questions!"

Whose job is it to make words come alive? It's the teacher's job. I have great faith in kindergartners. However, I worry what will happen to those children who love words when they enter the workbook-structured world of the first grade — a world of consonant sounds, long vowels, and short vowels. Unfortunately, it's too often a world where a magic circle melts away.

It was fun when you would visit us. I liked the first day you came and we picked the name Mr. Question. Another thing I

*liked was the circle where one person would stand and tell us
words they remember. I used to hide under my blanket, let my
head and hands hang down, and tease my brother and sisters that
I was a pachyderm. I would run around the house making noises
like a chanticleer. Sometimes I talk so much my mouth is full of
saliva. We have many birds in our yard. Some of the birds have
beautiful pinions.*

Margaret Keane, 1965

*I still remember some of the words you taught me like Apiristion
— gost, Chantacler — roster, pacadern — elephant, shapo — hat.
We actted out thease words like roster we went cock-a-do-dl-do.
It was so much fun learning and actting out the words.*

Ruth Herron, 1965

*I liked Mr. Question very much. He said funny things and he
answered our questions. Some were funny and strange.*

Caroline Ferris, 1965

Book Blabs

THE PHRASE "BOOK BLAB" sounds terribly non-intellectual, but actually Book Blabs proved to be hot-beds of controversy — literary controversy!

In this day of great stress upon individualized reading and individualized growth, which, of course, is highly commendable, there is also an urgent need to bring groups together occasionally. Forget individual projects, forget individual needs and rates of speed in reading, and present a common challenge to the whole class — a Book Blab!

One school year I conducted four exciting Book Blabs. One group, consisting of four sixth-grade classes, discussed Robert Louis Stevenson's *Black Arrow,* the famous western, *The Ox-Bow Incident,* Sherwood Anderson's play, *Abe Lincoln in Illinois,* and Admiral Peary's account of his voyage to the South Pole entitled *Zero.*

My selection of these works was based on the following three criteria:

1. I liked the books.
2. I knew the books thoroughly.
3. They cost only 60¢ in paperback form. The students invested their own money since I had not budgeted this item in June of the previous school year. (The idea hadn't occurred to me until two hours after Labor Day.)

The children were excited when the first book, *The Ox-Bow Incident*, arrived, and they began reading immediately that morning. The whole English period was a silent one, but tremendous energy was expended poring through the pages. It was a good beginning, and the youngsters finished reading the novel at home. Paperback books in hip pockets were a pleasant sight.

Not all the parents at first sensed the value of such a project.

"Is this a sixth-grade-level book, Mr. Cullum?" asked one mother.

"You must be kidding about not requiring a book report!" quipped another parent.

"What is this Book Blab nonsense?" inquired a third.

I invited them all to the Book Blab to be held in a few days, and I assured them that if my plan was not successful I would drop the whole idea. I wondered that night how they could have such little faith in their children.

What is a Book Blab? A Book Blab is a group of students gathered in an auditorium discussing the pros and cons of a book. The sessions were held after school, yet

75 per cent of the sixth-graders attended. Why? They came because it was exciting to share an opinion, exciting to disagree with another student, exciting to prove one's point, but most of all, it is always exciting to be associated with greatness.

Sometimes adults do not sense the touch of greatness, or perhaps they feel threatened by it and reject such an atmosphere. But children are always eager to embrace greatness, not because they comprehend its depth, but simply because there is always an aura of excitement about greatness. There is always a mystery and a strength!

The Book Blabs began at 3:30 p.m. and sometimes lasted until 5:30 p.m. Some students at first found it difficult to grasp that they were not required to attend.

"I have a piano lesson at 3:30," stated Nancy.

"I promised my dad I'd rake the lawn," said Ted.

"My mother wants me to go shopping with her," commented Gail.

"I signed up for after-school sports and the gym teacher will get mad if I miss it," explained Jimmy.

I reassured them over and over that Book Blabs were conducted on a volunteer basis and were not a school situation but a fun situation.

A group of children made a huge poster advertising the Book Blab with the name of the book, the date, and announcing that it was open to the public. Many parents were there that first October afternoon, and what was particularly delightful to me was to see several primary children sitting there waiting to see what was going to happen. I couldn't help but think that there were my book blabbers of the future.

I asked for some volunteers to join me on the panel at the long table on the apron of the stage. About seven volunteered. At first the students were hesitant about participating. After all, this was their first Book Blab. I started the proceedings by declaring, "Today we are gathered to discuss that famous western, *The Ox-Bow Incident*, one of my favorite books. Who wants to start the discussion? Anyone on the panel? Anyone from the floor?"

There was a buzzing about the audience. What should they say? What should they talk about? Where should they begin?

As all good teachers do when children are hesitant, the focus not clear to them, and they are afraid to expose themselves, the teacher earns his or her salary by assuming leadership. This was a situation where children needed a teacher's creative structure.

I began the discussion by telling them about an experience I had had with the actions of a mob. Years ago when I was twelve, I took my six-year-old brother to a Saturday afternoon movie. It was *Alice in Wonderland*. The lobby of the movie house was jammed with kids, all holding their dimes anxiously waiting to enter to find a good seat. A rumor spread around the lobby that there wouldn't be enough seats to accommodate everyone, and unfortunately when the usher opened only one door, everyone started to push. In the pushing I lost hold of my brother's hand, and there was nothing I could do to prevent him from being trampled. He and other children started crying, and I have never forgotten the terror of that mob violence incident. Luckily nothing serious happened, and we all had a pleasant three hours with Alice.

My little tale started the discussion rolling.

"It's a horrible thing when a group of kids gang up against one student," stated Ralph.

"Worse than that is when a group of girls out of sheer meanness keep another girl out of a group," said Carol.

Eventually the discussion rolled around to the mob violence of *The Ox-Bow Incident* where a group of people decide that three men are guilty and hang them without a legal trial, only later to discover the men were innocent. The students liked the novel and had become very emotionally involved in the situation. We did not discuss the literary style of the book, nor the vocabulary encountered, nor whether it was easy to read; that afternoon we discussed the emotional impact of *The Ox-Bow Incident* and the grave injustice of the whole affair.

Almost everyone volunteered some bit of discussion, and when they left the auditorium, they left with a satisfied feeling of having made a contribution. Not one student questioned the purpose, value, goals, or aims of our first Book Blab. It was simply a gathering together to discuss a book — no one was evaluated or graded.

A few months later we gathered for our second Book Blab. This time we gathered to exchange ideas about Stevenson's *Black Arrow*. There was no hesitancy about beginning the discussion this time.

"This was the most complicated novel I have ever read," complained Ann.

Others suggested that it was exciting but difficult to follow, so right then and there about seventy-five students started to reconstruct the plot. There was disagreement about what incident came first and who was on what side, but by five o'clock the story had been arranged in the correct order. The whole afternoon was similar to putting a huge jigsaw puzzle together. We discussed the unexpected aspects of the story, such as an arrow whizzing through the air and a character falling dead. It did not disturb me that the children found the plot a complicated one. The value of the afternoon lay in thinking the whole thing through together and some of the students reading the book a second time.

Abe Lincoln in Illinois stirred up considerable discussion. For the very first time students recognized a "weak" side of Lincoln. Many were sorry that their image of Lincoln had become slightly tarnished, but one of the students summed up the situation magnificently, "No one is perfect!"

On a Saturday afternoon two weeks later the group went to New York City where we saw the play *Abe Lincoln in Illinois*.

Our final Book Blab was based on Admiral Peary's *Zero*. The children had such admiration for that explorer. Over and over they repeated how almost impossible it was to do what he did!

Book Blabs exposed students to the joys of reading. One of the main jobs of a school is to instill a love of reading, and this is not done through phonics, book reports, outlining, summer reading lists, quizzes, grades, or having children take comprehension tests. A love of reading is developed through students and teachers sharing what they have read. The teacher should share with the student as if he or she has just read *Hamlet, Tom Sawyer,* or *The Three Little Pigs* for the very first time. Once a teacher loses the feeling of doing something for the first time, it is time for that teacher to change grades, schools, or profession.

If the Book Blabs were a success after school, imagine how effective they would be during the normal school day. Imagine not requiring book reports, but simply reading a book a month and discussing the book together. Imagine that ten books were read and discussed during the year and that during the final week of school the students suggested what books should be kept on the list for next year's class and what books should be dropped. That kind of curriculum development makes sense to me.

To break the ice you started to ask us questions concerning our opinions about the plot and theme and certain central characters. It was great because we all got to voice our opinions and say exactly what we thought. None of us could say anything without giving a reason for it, however, so we had to think and make sensible statements. There was quite a controversy over the book The Ox-Bow Incident. *Many parents didn't think that the book was a good choice for children, because in the beginning it had some swear words. The words weren't that bad and we had all heard them or would at some time in our life, so that was a foolish argument.*

Louise Lipman, 1963

The Book Blabs were a good idea. To read a book is only half the job. The other half is to be able to utilize the thoughts and ideas of the author. When all the sixth-graders got together to discuss one book, the second half of the job was being done.

Coline Jenkins, 1963

Geography Launchings

"CLOSE YOUR BOOKS EVERYONE! Close your eyes and listen. At the moment I'm in the Nutmeg State ready to leave for the Mohave Desert. After visiting my nephew, I travel to Mt. Rainier, Okeefenokee Swamp, and then to Lincoln's grave. I end my trip in the area of the United States that has the heaviest rainfall. Now, who is the detective who followed me from place to place without losing track of me?"

The fifth-grade class woke up! A dull period of social studies became an adventure hunt. The students wanted more. When I ran out of ideas, they made up their own puzzlers. What fun it was to lose a friend some place in the United States.

Nine-, ten-, and eleven-year-olds loved this approach to geography, and they realized that to participate they had to know their facts. They read their social studies book with an entirely new approach that had nothing to do with grades or tests but the inner excitement of a game well played!

Some educator once told me that fun was outdated methodology. How wrong he was, for fun will never be outdated. More important than anything else is *not how we teach,* but *what they learn.* If an elementary school is lacking excitement and the inner energy of fun, it might as well close up the store!

Another animated program was evolved around launchings into geographical space — all done on a volunteer basis. The children made up their own teams and elected their own captains. The class had five teams, five students on a team, and they competed against themselves, or if they chose, challenged another team.

One team called The London Company volunteered to launch itself into the New England area, which meant it would see how quickly it could locate twenty-five geographical locations correctly. The classroom was divided into six major areas representing the six New England states: Maine, New Hampshire, Vermont, Massachusetts, Connecticut, and Rhode Island.

The London Company lined up ready to go with its captain at the head of the line, for he would be the first to go into action. Team members took turns answering my set of questions, which I read one at a time. The official timekeeper announced, "Ten . . . nine . . . eight . . . seven . . . six . . . five . . . four . . . three . . . two . . . one . . . zero . . . and BLAST OFF!"

1. *Locate the famous cranberry bogs.*
Like a flash the captain raced to the part of the room that represented Massachusetts and placed a #1.
2. *Locate the New England state that does not have an Atlantic Ocean seaport.*

The next member of the team raced to the area of the room that was labeled Vermont and placed a #2.

3. *Locate the Aroostook Plain.*

The next team member started with a rush, but then hesitated. He raised his hand, which meant he was seeking aid from a team member. Into space plunged someone else on the team and identified the answer as Maine.

No child was embarrassed about asking for help. At the end of the twenty-five questions, The London Company finished in two minutes and forty-seven seconds.

Other teams attempted a launching of New England. Some were more successful, some not quite so successful. We also launched teams into the Southeastern states, Middle Atlantic states, Prairie states, Southwestern states, Rocky Mountain states, the provinces of Canada, and the countries of Central and South America. By the end of the school year those launchings made us authorities on the geography of the Western Hemisphere.

Books give different names for regional groupings of states, but the excitement of a geography launching will be exactly the same in southern South Carolina or a classroom in northern North Dakota. Of course there will be screams as the excitement builds up, and perhaps a student will fall from her "capsule" as she scampers about the room, but the temporary hurt of a bruised knee is worth involving students with political maps, graphic-relief maps, populations, capitals, annual rainfalls, altitudes, and so on.

I composed some of the questions for the launchings, and the students composed some. We did not limit ourselves to the basic class textbook with its workbook but also delved into the library atlas and the atlas in the attics at home. We read maps and many books, and we also kept our eyes on the local newspaper to see what current events could take us to various parts of the good old U.S.A.

Elementary schools could kick their scholastic legs even higher without any harm being done. Simply be sure to close your classroom door to hold down the noise, and your world of geography will thrive. Sometimes, however, even with the door closed, the fever of the excitement spreads. Boys and girls will talk! Certain teams held meetings after school or on Saturdays to review their strategy for their launchings of the next group of states.

Mastering the geography of North America was no longer dull school work but an experience of greatness. We traveled with such speed and such confidence that for the first time in years I was able to cover Canada, Mexico, and all of South America all the way to Tierra del Fuego!

I guess we were having too much success, for a formal protest was made to the principal by another fifth-grade teacher who stated that I was not fully covering the subject matter required by the curriculum. At first I saw red, but then I thought, "What a wonderful opportunity to prove that my method is a good one. Maybe not better, but certainly just as good as that utilized in the dull, quiet, sun-filtered classroom next door!"

The principal agreed to give every fifth-grade class a test based on geographical concepts of the Western Hemisphere. The day arrived. The test was given in the auditorium by the principal, and the tests were corrected by the principal. The results were gratifying, to say the least:

My room — an average of 95% accuracy
Teacher A — an average of 86% accuracy
Teacher B — an average of 79% accuracy
Teacher who complained — an average of 64% accuracy

But better than scoring highest was the evidence that my method worked. How could I ever doubt the excitement of nine-, ten-, and eleven-year-olds? They don't fake excitement — they don't know how.

I used this same geographic launching technique with a sixth-grade at St. Luke's school. We covered the Eastern Hemisphere in record style and ended with a finale that was unforgettable! We organized a series of panel discussions with eleven-year-old volunteers, and we invited the community to attend our geographic discussions, which were scheduled as follows:

May 10	Scandinavian Europe	4 p.m.
May 11	U.S.S.R.	7:30 p.m.
May 12	Central Europe	4 p.m.
May 13	Western Industrial Europe	7:30 p.m.
May 14	Mediterranean Europe	4 p.m.
May 17	Southwestern Asia	4 p.m.
May 18	India and Ceylon	7:30 p.m.
May 19	Southeastern Asia	4 p.m.
May 20	Eastern Asia	7:30 p.m.
May 21	Australia and New Zealand	4 p.m.

The biggest crowd attended the U.S.S.R. session. The five panelists marched into the room, took their places on the platform, and began the proceedings. Joel, the chairman, began by explaining the huge papier-mâché map the class had made of the Eastern Hemisphere. It was a bold map with vivid colors — almost an abstract painting. Each panelist made a short introductory speech explaining how he had become an expert in his field, and then an exchange of questions and answers started among the panelists. This, of course, was not rehearsed.

At first the adult guests didn't believe the panel chairman when he said, after an hour or so of discussion, "We now will answer all questions based on geography that you may wish to ask. It is obvious that we cannot answer questions of a historical nature, for that is too complicated for us at this time, and the purpose of these gatherings is geographic in nature, not historical."

The guests were surprised at such poise and confidence. They didn't realize that all this poise and confidence stemmed from a tremendous amount of reading and research. Actually the Eastern Hemisphere had been the focus of the reading program for the year — without a workbook!

I remained in the back of the classroom during all the sessions and only interfered when a question from the floor seemed to be unfair. After all, I had to protect my eleven-year-old geographic authorities from adults who enjoy tearing down rather than building up. Sometimes we teachers also tear down more than we build up.

If a question from the floor was unfair or completely out of place, I simply shook my head "No," and the chairman of that particular session would step in and announce, "We are not prepared to answer that question at this time. Perhaps with further research we might be able to help you." or "That question deals with history, and we are here to discuss only geography."

Those two weeks of panel discussions were two weeks of success and two weeks of greatness.

My friends, the custodians, complained about the evening sessions lasting past nine o'clock, for that's when they went home. They didn't want to stay overtime. I told them not to worry, that the kids would talk twice as fast during the evening sessions.

Try a geographic launching with your class! You never know where your capsule may land!

I remember distinctly the social studies races in which my team, The Five Explorers, set a new record, which as far as I know still stands.

Chris Ley, 1962

One of the group projects I remember was the eight-foot papier-mâché map of the United States. I was personally responsible for putting in the Great Lakes. If I didn't do them, they wouldn't exist. That was the feeling I had. And when I finished them they looked more beautiful to me than I could have thought possible. It was the teamwork that was thrilling. Boys have to learn teamwork automatically when they do sports, but girls don't. They don't learn the excitement of doing a little bit well with other people to get a large project well done. Hooray the Great Lakes!

Elspeth Woodcock, 1948

You employed the unique ingredient of fun into the lessons. This was especially true of the geography races we staged in the classroom. In these races you didn't just have to know a fact, you had to know it fast.

Cathy Coshal, 1962

Reading Workbooks or
Reading Shakespeare?

THE ELEMENTARY SCHOOL is the ideal place to introduce Shakespeare. I have been challenged on this position many times by teachers who decry the evils of presenting Shakespeare too early, but I say, "Find someone else with whom to debate the issue, for I am convinced since I have been introducing Shakespeare to kindergartners and elementary school children for the last twenty years, and my students have embraced this playwright later in high school and college. Many have thanked me for the early introduction to William."

Shakespeare may be for scholars to debate and discuss and philosophize over, but he is also for Corky, a fifth-grader who died beautifully as Julius Caesar. There are "murderers" galore in the elementary schools ready to help Macbeth kill Banquo; many a fifth- and sixth-grade girl can really whip up a moment of insanity as Ophelia.

Kindergarten is the perfect time to acquaint children with the greatness of Shakespeare. It is so simple for a kindergarten teacher to become a Queen Titania or a King Oberon and gather his or her five-year-old fairies in the magic forest of *A Midsummer Night's Dream*; it is so simple for a first-grade teacher to bring into his classroom a pot with some dry ice and a little bit of water and create an atmosphere for the weird sisters with the chant:

> Double, double toil and trouble;
> Fire burn and cauldron bubble. . . .

The teacher will soon be pushed aside and replaced by six-year-old Shakespearean witches.

It is so simple for a third-grade teacher to introduce *Julius Caesar* by letting his children pretend to be the fickle, violent crowd. There's not a classroom in the country that will be able to resist the intrigue of the line from *Hamlet*:

> The play's the thing
> Wherein I'll catch the conscience of the king.

No one loses his place when the murder scene of King Duncan from *Macbeth* is being read in whispers; no one is daydreaming when Juliet Capulet hesitates to drink the liquid that will make her appear dead; no one is looking at the clock when the two very young royal princes are ushered into the Tower of London to their death.

Once a kindergarten class attended a condensed performance of *The Taming of the Shrew*, which was given by a sixth-grade class, and the arguing and bickering on stage reminded the little ones of their family life. When I visited them the following year when they were first-graders and asked them what story they wanted to hear, the response was *The Taming of the Shrew*. Why?

They simply wanted to laugh again! School kids come to school to laugh, to be scared, to daydream, to take revenge.

Children learn to read by pursuing the activities of Dick, Jane, and Spot, but once they have mastered the skill of reading, why keep them with that dull dog and those dull children? Why not expose them to the classics?

Don't let *your* fears of the classics spill out upon children. Don't limit a child's world! When children acquire a taste of Shakespeare, they actively live with each of his situations and become involved. They thirst for more. Give them a taste of greatness in elementary school; then the high schools can really and truly explore.

The elementary school is the place to feed imaginations not yet cluttered with personal problems. Let's stop feeding kids second-rate stuff. Children quickly outgrow phrases such as "I see Dick. . . . Dick has a dog," and respond to such expressions as:

> A horse! A horse! My kingdom for a horse!

> or

> Yond Cassius has a lean and hungry look;
> He thinks too much: such men are dangerous.

Teachers will be thoroughly surprised how elementary school children relish the excitement and conniving of these famous Shakespearean lines.

Skeptical teachers always ask, "But do they really understand what they are reading and saying?" My answer is that some students understand all, some almost all, and some half of all! What are schools for but to expand the horizons of students as far as they will go? I haven't heard of a student who died from being challenged, but I've heard of many who wasted away from boredom.

Suppose all of a sudden the reading programs of the fourth, fifth, and sixth grades became difficult and challenging? What would happen? The only thing that would happen would be that the teacher would have to explain more complex vocabulary and structure rather than correct another set of workbooks, student-teacher discussions would evolve, the content of stories would be explored in more depth, and there would be involvement, interest, and a personal feeling of success on both sides of the teacher's desk.

There are two aspects to every classroom—the students and the teacher! Both need to be touched by greatness. Students seek for the mystery and magic of school that was there the first day they entered the hallowed halls. Give them the magic and mystery again . . . it is so easy to do!

Teachers don't have to be good actors and actresses— just themselves. Forget your inhibitions and dare to experiment. In creative work, children will respond only when their teachers are relaxed, free, and truly themselves. Why should children reveal themselves when a teacher doesn't? Make a Lady Macbeth and her bloody hands come to life. Describe the doubts of a tormented Hamlet. Allow Ariel to fly about the classroom.

Since one can't start children with too large a dose, how does a teacher establish the exciting atmosphere of Shakespeare in an elementary school classroom? Simply choose a Shakespearean play that *you* like and *tell* your class the story. You will sense the silence of involvement as you spin the tale of the magical moonlight of *A Midsummer Night's Dream*, or tell about the enchanted island inhabited by a magician and a monster in *The Tempest*, or relate the foul deed done on a dark night in Scotland and spilling of blood in *Macbeth*, or recount the story of the evil hunchback king and the shadow of the Tower of London in the world of *Richard III*.

When you and the children have become absorbed, then is the time to set aside the basal reader and its workbook and substitute a scene or a few scenes from your favorite Shakespearean play.

Through years of experimenting with elementary school classrooms, I have discovered that of the thirty-six plays written by William Shakespeare, nine are suitable for elementary school reading curriculums, progressive or traditional. These nine plays are:

Macbeth (tragedy)	4-5-6th grades
Julius Caesar (tragedy)	4-5-6th grades
Comedy of Errors (comedy)	4-5-6th grades
Hamlet (tragedy)	5-6th grades
Romeo and Juliet (tragedy)	5-6th grades
The Taming of the Shrew (comedy)	5-6th grades
A Midsummer Night's Dream (comedy)	5-6th grades
The Tempest (comedy)	6th grade
Richard III (history)	6th grade

Perhaps you will disagree with my ratings; perhaps you will wish to add *As You Like It* or *The Merchant of Venice* . . . fine!

You will discover that your reading groups or the whole class will want to read Shakespearean scenes over and over again. Each time a play is reread, switch the roles about. This is the ideal time to spot a shy child on the verge of volunteering to be a noble Brutus, a confused Queen Gertrude, or a comical nurse.

Often my reading groups have requested that their reading of a play be taped. What excitement has permeated the classroom as we prepared to listen to the taped performance. Many students have come back after school to listen again and again.

After you have read the plays and taped them, perhaps you and your reading groups are ready to stage one. How? Very simple. The magic and miracle of children will carry the play.

The first obstacle to overcome is that of scenery. Scenery is completely unnecessary. A platform here and a platform there will suffice, and in case you don't have platforms, the words of William Shakespeare and the imagination of young actors and actresses will be quite sufficient.

What about costumes and props? Anything that cannot be prepared simply and quickly by a child is absolutely non-essential. In a recent production of *Macbeth*, the boy playing Macbeth forgot the daggers with which he had killed King Duncan. When Lady Macbeth asked, "Why did you bring these daggers from the place? They must lie there!" not one person in the audience noticed that Macbeth was not holding any daggers. In fact, even Macbeth himself didn't realize the daggers were missing.

The world of the elementary school can be a success world, for every child at this stage has some talent. Children are honest and direct in their interpretations, so there are few problems about acting or directing. By the way, let boys or girls play any part. My best Mark An-

tonys have been girls, and my best *A Midsummer Night's Dream* production was put on by an all-boy cast. All a teacher has to do is to expose elementary school children to greatness, and they will speak their lines with the confidence of a Gielgud and the energy of a Judith Anderson.

As an example, here's a summary of the way a production of *Julius Caesar* was evolved, fourth-grade style. First we rehearsed in the classroom on a most informal basis, and as structure and confidence developed, we transferred our creative energy to the auditorium.

SCENE 1

A boy stepped in front of the curtain, raised his sword, and announced to the audience: "Get ye off the streets. This is a day in honor of Caesar. Clear the streets for Caesar comes soon!"

SCENE 2

The curtain slowly opened on a dark stage. Everyone was in his place. Caesar was on a wooden platform with Brutus on his right and Mark Antony on his left; the crowd was in a formal position facing the audience. The lights slowly rose as a roll of drums was heard.

The soothsayer spoke. I like to use all parts of an auditorium, so from the rear was intoned the famous line, "Beware the Ides of March!" Caesar ignored this advice and left the stage with his entourage.

SCENE 3

Cassius and Brutus appeared alone, and Cassius planted the seeds of doubt in Brutus' good ear. Here the play actually began.

SCENE 4

I slashed the approximately eleven conspirators down to three for fourth-graders. Shakespeare wouldn't have minded, as long as the kids knew that in the original there are many more than three.

Cassius and Casca plotted the death of Caesar. Then they threw a rock through the window of Brutus' house to persuade him to become more involved. The note on the rock said, "Brutus, thou sleepest. Awake and see thy self! Shall Rome stand under one man's rule? Speak! Strike!"

SCENE 5

Portia, the wife of Brutus, also awakened by the noise, appeared in her nightgown (Roman toga). She pleaded with her noble husband to confide in her. He refused to divulge the secret plans.

SCENE 6

Calpurnia, Caesar's wife, pleaded with Caesar not to go to the Senate for she had had a terrible nightmare. Caesar ignored her warning and went to the Senate.

Does it sound terribly complicated to have a scene in the house of Brutus and then a few minutes later a scene in the house of Caesar? It's very simple! All one does is make two signs and pin them to the curtain. On one side of the stage in front of the curtain will be a sign saying "House of Brutus" and on the other side of the stage a sign, "House of Caesar."

SCENE 7

How to kill Caesar? Easy! To avoid real bloodshed and to prevent turning the play into a comedy, have Caesar killed with a sort of slow-motion action, with dull lights and the roll of a drum. Children today are sophisticated. We must give them a touch of the theatrical to help them enrich their fantasies.

Each conspirator slowly walked up to Caesar, plunged in a knife, and pulled out the knife. Caesar held his position as did the others, and when Brutus stabbed his best friend, the drum stopped and Caesar uttered the spine-tingling words, "Et tu, Brute!"

The crowd panicked at the sight of blood and ran out in all directions. (Everyone likes to practice this part over and over again.)

SCENE 8

Mark Antony made a dramatic appearance. Kneeling at Caesar's body he cried, "Oh mighty Caesar, dost thou lie so low?" He persuaded the conspirators to permit him to speak at Caesar's funeral.

Brutus spoke to the crowd first. It had returned to the auditorium and now stood in the orchestra pit, pounding on the apron of the stage demanding satisfaction! Brutus stepped out to the footlights, silenced the crowd, and spoke. Mark Antony then stepped out, changed the mood of the crowd, and inspired them to fury and destruction. The auditorium was pitch black by then, and the crowd lighted their torches. (The kids can use flashlights covered with red cellophane. This device always works!)

I usually end the play with the words spoken by Mark Antony: "Now let it work. Mischief thou art afoot. Take thou what course thou wilt!"

The play is a hit every time, and the kids want to do it again and again.

The words and thoughts of the great dramatist have never failed to interest elementary school children, and I have yet to see a group of elementary school children who did not capture the spirit and beauty of William Shakespeare.

When three boys can wrap themselves in a front curtain and convince an audience that they are murderers waiting for Banquo, their class is a productive, imaginative one; when stupid servants in *The Taming of the Shrew* cover their faces thinking they are escaping the wrath of Petruchio, that is creative thinking; when a nine-year-old, who is in the second reading group, can interpret the role of Juliet with sensitivity and grace, something's wrong with the reading program; and when kids can attempt to discuss and compare Richard Burton's interpretation of Hamlet to that of their friend, eleven-year-old David, all is right with that school world.

I was so involved in the play Macbeth, *I can remember actually donning my Macduff costume under my clothes one day to appear as a "Super-MacDuff" in case of an emergency! My mother didn't appreciate that!*

Eddie Balls, 1958

One of the greatest things that you gave your students was the realization that learning could be fun. Through things like poetry and literature festivals we learned to appreciate the Eng-

lish language. To this day I could still act out my part as the Soothsayer in Julius Caesar, *and without much practice either. I still remember the feeling of excitement that you directed into us when we did the crowd scene at the end of Antony's speech . . . our running across a glowing red stage screaming and carrying smoking sticks and clubs.*

Kenneth Packer, 1957

The experiences were great. We had to make our own costumes and use whatever little props we could dig up. Being able to talk in front of large audiences has become very helpful in high school. My greatest challenge was playing Juliet in Shakespeare's Romeo and Juliet.

Patty Kohlasch, 1959

The most lasting effect, I think, of my work with you is that it made Shakespeare come alive and made it fun.

John Light, 1964

The most important effect of the whole Shakespeare experiences with Mr. Cullum was the introduction it provided to the works of Shakespeare. It was thoroughly enjoyable, and more important, I find my understanding of Shakespeare when I now read it in prep school to be much greater, and the plays seem more significant and vital.

Robert Elmore, 1961

King Tut's Tomb

IT WAS FRIGHTENING at times to stumble accidentally face-first into a cobweb, but it certainly made learning the basic skills of arithmetic much more palatable. Problem-solving, double division, or inverting fractions in the basement of St. Luke's Chapel choir room made arithmetic a fascinating "happening."

What do cobwebs and excitement, and even flashlights, have to do with learning arithmetic? Everything!

When I was a fifth- and sixth-grade teacher at the old St. Luke's School in Greenwich Village, I was assigned the room known as the choir room. The choir room had a trap door. Of course the class opened the trap door and climbed down to explore the cellar, which some have considered to be part of the old burial ground of St. Luke's Chapel. It was dark and damp down there, and the children hoped someone would actually find a human bone. This is where the arithmetic "digs" originated.

Approximately once a week, I opened the trap door so that the children could explore for arithmetic problems. The night before I had visited the "tomb" and had scattered problems about. The arithmetic challenges were typed on index cards of different sizes, and each card was labeled according to the difficulty of its problem. As the children wandered about, they inadvertently stumbled upon index cards and commenced to work the problems and the puzzles. Everyone loved arithmetic!

The cellar was spooky, but not so spooky that the students couldn't concentrate. When a child had solved his problem, he scrambled up to daylight and presented me with a dusty but completed problem. Some problems were worth as much as fifty points.

All digs were successful, for each student had his or her own level of competence, and each decided what his level of success would be for each day. This technique seemed to relax everyone, for some days one would be more ambitious than others.

Drilling and reviewing seem to take up so much time in elementary classrooms, but they do not have to be boring. Children learn better when they're excited and talkative rather than composed and quiet. Opening that trap door in the St. Luke's Chapel choir room exposed the children to a fresh breath of a mysterious damp, stale air, but arithmetic was learned!

Years later when working as a fifth-grade teacher at Midland School in Rye, I did not teach arithmetic one session. Miss Mones, the teacher across the hall, did teach it, and she seemed to be searching for a new approach to arithmetic review. My memory was refreshed by that breath of fresh, damp, stale air. I mentioned to Miss Mones the success I had with my St. Luke's School arithmetic digs, and she, a courageous soul, was willing to gamble. What was there to lose? Nothing really.

This was the beginning of King Tut's Tomb. At first the tomb consisted of some sheets hung over a string attached to the walls with nails in a corner of the back of the room. All the time we were frightened that the project might be canceled because of the edict, "No nails in the walls!"

However, the principal of Midland School came to the rescue by helping develop a permanent structure for the tomb. The walls and roof consisted of large mattress boxes nailed and stapled onto a light weight wooden framework; a low door was cut through on one side. Life-sized figures, about six-feet high and made by the children, guarded the tomb. Each figure was beautifully detailed in the ancient Egyptian art form with modern poster paint, and the walls too were brightly painted. The entrance to the tomb was covered with a piece of black cloth.

The boys and girls were excited, just as the St. Luke's youngsters had been excited, just as any elementary school kid in any country would be excited. It's fascinating how a change of pace can intrigue the elementary school child, how a fresh breath of stale damp air in the atmosphere can cause a stir of wonder.

Did you ever hear of fifth-grade students working on math problems during their free time? It happened. Excitement built up while the tomb was being constructed.

The class read about Egyptian tombs and discussed Egyptian treasures and curses. Their imaginations were stirred to become archeologists.

What was the reason for a King Tut's Tomb? Math problems, puzzles, arithmetic challenges, graphs, and other items dealing with numbers and numerals were the treasures within King Tut's Tomb. The "archeologists" dug for the solutions.

Who was eligible to dig? Everyone. To become an archeologist and be able to dig in King Tut's Tomb one had to have the right attitude. What was the right attitude? The right attitude was the ability to be reliable and to be able to work independently.

The "cut-ups" presented something of a problem—would they be able to handle themselves properly inside the dark tomb? Could they conduct themselves as archeologists? Would they pinch, kick, or strike their colleagues in the dark or would they be so fascinated searching and stumbling for mathematical excitement that they would not be tempted to be unruly? I am happy to report that everyone behaved in an exemplary manner.

The mechanics of operating King Tut's Tomb were simple:

1. Problems for each dig were written on cards and tacked inside the tomb.
2. Each problem was given a point score, which was noted on the card. The more difficult or time-consuming ones were worth more. Since this project was not designed solely for able students, problems included simple computations as well as involved and difficult problems. There were puzzles, construction problems,

and all types of odds and ends. Here are some examples:

$$\frac{\frac{3}{4}}{\frac{5}{16}} \times 1 = ?$$

3469
2187
3412
+ 6110

Factor 1870 into prime factors.

How many hockey teams can be formed by the fourth-, fifth-, and sixth-grade boys' gym class if there are 58 boys in the class?

In the decimal numeral 4659.67:
    a. the 7 represents ———————
    b. the 4 represents ———————
    c. the 9. represents ———————

Represent 43 using Egyptian symbols.

What is the sum of CCCLXXVI and MDCCL?

Can you tell why zero is a multiple of every whole number?

3. Each problem was numbered and stayed in the tomb for others to "discover." Dig answers had to be turned in with a number; otherwise it became too complicated to score. The answers were deposited in a box designed as a sarcophagus. The reason for scoring was that to receive credit for a dig, each archeologist had to acquire a certain amount of points within the time of that particular dig.

4. Wrong answers were returned to be worked again if the student so wished.

5. A dig generally lasted about two weeks, and then the cards were taken down. Sometimes a difficult card that had stumped several kids stayed up for another dig.
6. After each dig, answers were discussed, and ways of approaching problems were exchanged. This was the valuable aspect of the project.
7. At the end of the year very fancy certificates were presented to the active, hardworking archeologists.

King Tut's Tomb captured the fancy of the children. Archeologists would drop in with flashlights, paper, and pencils and before entering King Tut's Tomb, each one was required to bow respectfully three times before the entrance. There were very few that didn't feel the spirit and catch the excitement. For some it was a temporary excitement; for others it lasted the whole year. Some just sensed the excitement in being admitted to the tomb by going through the rigmarole required to enter; others accepted the challenge of delving into a mystery. Some were reinforced by the majestic appearance of a King Tut's Tomb and were able to step into the unknown.

With the aid of flashlights and some synthetic grains of sand, students emerged from the tomb not only with a solved arithmetic problem but with another facet of their personalities successfully exposed.

The opening of the tomb for the first dig was announced over the school's loud speaker. This was done before each dig. The times when the tomb would be opened were announced. To accommodate eager diggers, the tomb was opened for digging before classes began in the morning, during class whenever anyone had some free time available, and after school.

After three o'clock was a busy time! Not too many teachers allowed their children to leave their respective classrooms during the day to visit the tomb, so those after-school archeologists made up for lost time. After bowing down on hands and knees, he or she would crawl into the tomb. Remember the entrance was low! No one could enter the tomb without performing the ritual. No one could enter who wouldn't comply with all the rules and regulations.

Teachers came from other schools to see what was happening. Some caught the spirit and bowed three times before entering; others, however, could not capture the world of make-believe, and they were not permitted to go in.

It was dark inside the tomb, darker than outside. Flashlights were used although they were not always essential. On winter afternoons though, the late diggers really did need them. They loved to work when it became dark. However, work on the problems could be done at home or at school or whenever an archeologist had time.

The back of the classroom always had an archeologist or two working on a problem. Some would always stay to watch Miss Mones empty the sarcophagus.

Parents began stopping by to see what this tomb was all about, for their youngsters were most involved with math puzzles, looking things up in the almanac, making hourglasses that ran for five minutes, and coming home with slightly soiled clothes. A few parents even bowed three times and crawled into King Tut's Tomb.

There were no grades connected with King Tut's Tomb — only a child's interest and perseverance were valued. Consequently the children worked independently. They chose their own problems, persisted if they were so inclined, or dropped the project.

The St. Luke's Chapel choir room still exists, but it is no longer used as a classroom, for St. Luke's School has a brand-new building. The Midland School King Tut's Tomb has been discarded, but there are a few hundred students throughout the country whose nostrils are still sensitive to a fresh breath of damp, dark, stale air.

Whether it be new math or old math, permit this fresh breath of damp, dark, stale air to enter your classroom.

The tomb made math fun and challenging, and something you didn't do just for grades or tests. Maybe this is one of the major reasons why math is my favorite subject today.

Beth Pomerantz, 1962

Before you went in, it was essential *that you bowed three times. This was for the benefit of King Tutankhamen himself. Getting help from other people was taboo; this was a do-it-yourself project. Even now I sort of feel a thrill when I think about the tomb, the darkness, and quiet inside penetrated by several flashlights. I'm sure I'll never forget it!*

Jon Lawson, 1962

Elementary School
Dancing Toes

IT ALL BEGAN with my St. Luke's School fourth-graders about twenty years ago. The girls in the class decided it would be fun to start their own ballet company and, of course, the first ballet in their repertoire would be their version of *Swan Lake*.

As director of the ballet company, I was not a qualified choreographer à la Balanchine or Robbins, but I was and am an ardent devotee of the dance. I thought, "Why not allow the girls themselves to establish some semblance of organization through their own choreography?"

I made a few suggestions, they made a few, and the St. Luke's School Ballet Company was born. The Tchaikowsky music swelled and diminished romantically while the girls lost most of their self-consciousness and created some intricate dance movements. Some of the girls imagined that they were prima ballerinas, but one little girl identified herself with the Radio City Music

Hall Rockettes. To each his own success level, as I have so often stated.

There was great excitement the day they first performed for the school. Their homemade costumes looked fine. They were of traditional white, consisting of white tops and white skirts that fell a few inches above the knee. Fourteen girls had such costumes, but a poor forlorn fifteenth girl wore her mother's petticoat, which came down to her ankles. The mother thought it immodest of her ten-year-old daughter to be dressed otherwise.

It was an interesting ensemble of fifteen swans with fifteen ostrich feathers held to their heads by thick rubber bands — and one girl with her mother's petticoat down to her ankles. However, the melancholy strains of Tchaikowsky's music soon swept us into the creative world of fourth-grade girls. Each girl kept her ostrich feather as a souvenir.

When I went to work for the Rye Public School System I introduced the Ballet Club to the third- to sixth-grade girls of Midland School. There was a large turnout on the first Friday after school when all types of girls auditioned. Some of the more aggressive young ladies danced very sophisticated and spontaneous steps to the *Symphony in C* by Bizet, while the very shy ones barely moved. The girls always auditioned in groups rather than alone and, of course, everyone passed the audition and became a full-fledged member of the Midland School Ballet Club.

The ballets through the years ranged from autumn leaves falling to the ground to a ballet depicting the meanness of a group toward an individual. I shall always

remember Eugenia's fifth-grade interpretation of the not-wanted girl. The pleading movements of her arms and body were emotional spontaneity at its best. Wagner's *Tristan and Isolde* music helped the cause.

Perhaps the high point of the ballet years at Midland School occurred the day five boys slowly but firmly entered the auditorium and asked to be members of the club. At first the girls laughed, but I quickly explained that there was nothing wrong with boys or men dancing. I explained that great athletes have the grace and agility of dancers and quite often football coaches prescribe dancing exercises for the players to improve their balance. The boys did not perform for the public, but they certainly received a workout at our Friday afternoon sessions.

The highlight of the Midland School Ballet Club came the year Rye celebrated its 300th birthday anniversary in 1960. Dr. James J. Collins, the principal, asked me to think of a way in which Midland School could be part of that celebration. I decided to use the Midland School Ballet Club as the main structure of a gigantic circus, and it was some circus! Almost every boy and girl joined the Ballet Club. It practically had a cast of thousands! The Friday after-school rehearsals from 3:30 to 5 p.m. were exhausting to anyone over twenty-one, but fun!

Finally the day in April arrived when the 300th anniversary celebration commenced. That was a red-letter day for me, for it was the first and only time I ever saw a curriculum fade into the background, for Dr. Collins allowed the circus participants to forget classes and present three performances in one day. The morning performance was for the primary children of the school and visiting

schools, the afternoon performance was for the older children and visiting schools, and the evening performance was for the adult world. Even the mayor attended.

First, fifth-grade Martin, dressed as a hobo clown, warmed up the audience with some comical antics of sweeping the stage before he turned loose approximately forty other clowns of all types. There were the lost clowns who cried and cried as they searched for their way, led by fifth-graders Chuck and Ira. Stephen was a cigar-smoking baby-carriage clown; Chris, Bill, and numerous others were white clowns who danced about the audience cracking jokes and chatting with the spectators.

Huge elephants danced, controlled by their tiny fifth-grade trainer, Louise; Debbie, Jeanne, and her brother Mark were playful dogs; sixth-grader Lori and fifth-grader Lacey did a leopard-panther dance. It was wild!

Jimmy was the leader of the jungle dance that involved fifteen other boys; Beth and Francia of the fifth grade did a delightful snake dance. I also danced in the role of a ballerina gorilla, ably assisted by two fourth-grade ballerinas, Elizabeth and Patty. I chose them as my partners for they were petite and easy to lift.

Miss Mones, a fifth-grade teacher, was an old lady with two dozen children underneath her huge skirt. Paul, a fourth-grader, tightroped along the edge of the stage balanced by a tiny umbrella. Horses entered the auditorium arena with real live knights on their backs. There was much dancing, mixed with a dash of running and jumping, and there was very much sincerity and involvement.

When the circus trains pulled away never to return, a small group of mothers decided that the Midland School

Ballet Club à la Cullum could be improved upon, and basically they were right. They hired a professional dance teacher to conduct classes at Midland School once a week. I naturally disbanded my group to avoid friction. Some of the girls joined the new organization and learned the correct way to dance, "with a one and two and three and four, and one and two and three and four, and one and two and . . ." but none of my fat girls joined and most of my shy ones did not return for the second week of perfection.

The St. Luke's School and Midland School Ballet Clubs were not training the nine-, ten-, and eleven-year-old girls for the New York City Ballet or the Bolshoi but simply giving them an opportunity to express themselves through body movement — perhaps a chance to dream for a moment!

A few years later I started the Osborn School Ballet Club with much moral support from William E. Turner, the principal. We presented a program entitled "Poetry and the Dance" that was memorable. The girls worked Friday afternoons and Saturday afternoons until I was too tired to go on. What energy and creativity they possessed.

One of our big productions was an interpretation of Ralph Waldo Emerson's poem "Snowstorm." The girls were all in white costumes ranging from tennis outfits to tutus, to sheets, to white curtains, to pajamas. It was a madly whirling ballet of white and off-white involving sixty elementary school girls who were not counting one and two and three and four and one . . . but just dancing, jumping, and running, making believe they were Emersonian snowflakes. Memories of Penny as the bouncy, humorous snowflake are still with me as are the gracefulness of Priscilla and Karen. I could see that ballet every week, and the girls never tired of rehearsing it. It was truly a team effort.

We also staged a horse-race ballet based on the song poem "That Old Gray Mare She Ain't What She Used to Be." The eight horses were numbered, and the younger children in the audience screamed with delight as the horse for which they were cheering forged ahead. In our choreography, Charlotte, number 3, was the winner. It was fascinating to watch her weave in and out of the other horses and cross the finish line first. That's another ballet of which we never tired.

We ended our program with a spooky ballet based on James Whitcomb Riley's poem "Little Orphant Annie" and used the *Danse Macabre* music by Saint-Saëns. The audience looked forward to being scared and hearing the lines, "An' the Gobble-uns'll git you, ef you don't watch out!" There were wild screams from the ballerinas as well as the audience.

Through the years of working with elementary school girls, I, of course, realized that we were not performing ballet in its purest form. There was very little right but very little wrong. Their feet might not have been dancing, but their hearts certainly were.

My favorite thing I did with you was the dance festival. You let us dance the way we felt rather than teaching us step by step. I really liked this and felt I gained something out of it.

Jackie Borck, 1966

Before fifth grade, I had no real knowledge of the cultural world around me. Although I'm sure I wasn't able to comprehend the meanings of paintings or poetry or plays on a very deep level, nor was I able to dance in the ballet club like Martha Graham, it didn't matter. Mr. Cullum let each student enjoy culture at his own level, whether it was by two-stepping in a home-made petticoat or by listening to the sound of poetry.

Pam Reichert, 1960

In the after-school program the fourth-, fifth-, and sixth-grade girls of Osborn School presented a performance of spontaneous ballet. This was worthwhile! At one time we were butterflies, at another we were ghosts, and once we were Spanish dancers.

Lauren Hawkins, 1966

In our ballet class we made up dances to various music. It was great fun creating and making our costumes.

Susan Rosenstadt, 1965

Poetry Pot

A LARGE IRON CALDRON, if possible . . . a dash of water, if possible . . . a slab of dry ice, if possible. . . . Place all these in the front of the room on a desk, a platform, or some other elevated surface, add some steps to walk up and, with a defined ritual that all elementary school children love to accept, drop the spirit of a poet into the pot.

The ritual can be anything the children choose. It may be a trio of students kneeling before the caldron, it may be the class chanting the name of a poet or poetess, or it may be the closing of all eyes as the president of the class silently climbs the steps and drops a piece of dry ice into the water.

As the dry ice fumes rise, call, for example, upon the spirit of Edna St. Vincent Millay, and then and there, you the teacher, the exposer, can expose your class to the delicate thoughts of Miss Millay. I have shared some of my favorite Millay with many classes, reading the poems with much love and a sense of intimacy as if Miss Millay were actually in the room. Sometimes there was much discussion about a poem, and sometimes there was silence. I enjoyed the moments of silence. No, the children were not asleep — they were so completely involved they just could not talk. Both boys and girls responded to Miss Millay.

Of course, all children from six to eleven will not understand the full depth of Miss Millay, but they will understand her great sympathy and love for the fragile life of birds and animals. They will nod with understanding as you introduce:

> Black bird scudding
> Under the rainy sky,
> How wet your wings must be!
> And your small head how sleek and cold with water. . . .

In this poem Miss Millay shares her sadness with the bobolink. How many children have shared their sadness with animals to escape the harshness of every-day living? Miss Millay receives courage from the wet, cold bobolink and ends her poem by saying:

> Bobolink, you and I, an airy fool and an earthy
> Chuckling under the rain!
> *I shall never be sad again.*
> *I shall never be sad again.*
> Ah, sweet, absurd,
> Belovèd, bedraggled bird!

There is an urgent need for good poetry early in the elementary schools. Children have insight and understanding, and good poetry will inspire them to expose and share the greatness that is within themselves.

The spirit of Miss Millay can picture for them a fawn:

> There it was I saw what I shall never forget
> And never retrieve.
> Monstrous and beautiful to human eyes, hard to believe,
> He lay, yet there he lay,
> Asleep on the moss, his head on his polished cleft
>   small ebony hooves
> The child of the doe, the dappled child of the deer.
>
> Surely his mother had never said, "Lie here
> Till I return," so spotty and plain to see
> On the green grass lay he.
> His eyes had opened; he considered me. . . .

Every single child from IQ 73 to IQ 173 will look at you or the pot with the wisp of smoke, but their hearts will be reaching out to pet the fawn. A moment of quiet magic will be in your room — a touch of greatness will enter their lives.

> Was it alarm, or was it the wind of my fear lest
>   he depart
> That jerked him to his jointy knees,
> And sent him crashing off, leaping and stumbling
> On his new legs, between the stems of the white trees?

Although the fawn ran away, some of the children, whether Miss Millay knew it or not, had gently touched the fawn, some had even talked to the fawn, and to some the fawn had talked back.

The strong, delicate words of poets should be spoken in classrooms. Consider the excitement of Miss Millay warning the rabbit to beware of the hawk:

> Hop!
> Streak it for the bushes! Why do you sit so still?
> You are bigger than a house, I tell you, you are bigger
>   than a hill, you are a beacon for air-planes! . . .

Children relish such excitement, and no one is emotionally harmed when the hawk does kill the rabbit.

Once the sixth-grade girls of Midland School presented an after-school assembly program based on the poems of Edna St. Vincent Millay. Attendance and participation, as always, were voluntary. This was the school paper's review:

THE EDNA ST. VINCENT MILLAY POETRY RECITAL

Eight girls of Grade 6C presented the third Poetry Recital of the school year on Friday, March 23rd. The poems were those of Edna St. Vincent Millay.

There was a bare stage with a row of seven chairs and occasionally small props were used which gave an excellent effect. All the poems were memorized and were not announced. If the poems had been announced I feel it would have ruined the whole program.

The way the program was staged helped to reveal the beauty and variety of Millay's poetry. It was not done in the ordinary fashion of just one girl standing up to recite. Occasionally a few girls took different positions on the stage to say the poetry.

The girls participating were: Susan Hadley, Lelia Birrell, Cathy Robie, Joan Fenzi, Linda Sarles, Barbara Banister, and Diane Spearman.

Pam Roman told a little bit about Edna St. Vincent Millay at the beginning of the recital.

I would like to congratulate the girls for their marvelous performance. I was sorry that the recital lasted only a half-hour.

Helen Manuel, Drama Critic

One day the Poetry Pot sent up whiffs of real "corn." Fifth- and sixth-graders howled at some jokes of Carl

Sandburg, even though they were sophisticated young boys and girls. It was good to let their hair down as they laughed at:

> *Man:* Which way to the post office?
> *Girl:* I don't know.
> *Man:* You don't know much, do you?
> *Girl:* No, but *I* ain't lost.

> *Man:* Miss Jones, as you look over your 98 years, what gives you the greatest satisfaction?
> *Miss Jones:* Young man, you can tell your readers, the greatest satisfaction is that I haven't an enemy in the world.
> *Man:* That's a beautiful thought . . . not an enemy in the world.
> *Miss Jones:* Yes sir! I outlived them all!

Although the students roared and said "how corny," the Poetry Pot sent out the spirit of Mr. Sandburg and the greatness that helped him capture the spirit of Abe Lincoln. As the Poetry Pot boiled and bubbled, I read the class some of his words about Lincoln:

> Bells rang, there was a grinding of wheels, and the train moved, and carried Lincoln away from Springfield.
> The tears were not yet dry on some faces when the train had faded into the grey to the east.

Many of the children, on their own, looked into Sandburg's works about Lincoln. Of course, they did not read all the volumes, but a beginning was made.

The following day they truly understood the humanity of Carl Sandburg when they heard:

> Why did the children
> Put beans in their ears

When the one thing we told the children
They must NOT do
Was put beans in their ears?

Why did the children
Pour molasses on the cat
When the one thing we told the children
They must NOT do
Was pour molasses on the cat?

Through the mystery of the Poetry Pot and Carl Sandburg they met a cripple, they met Mildred Klinghoffer, bugs, a gray rat, and they met a poet they understood. They were touched by Carl Sandburg's greatness.

In the spring of 1965 three "poets" visited the Midland School. Carl Sandburg arrived with Robert Frost and Langston Hughes. The auditorium was jammed, naturally, for it is not often that three internationally famous poets visit a public school.

First Mr. Frost was presented to the audience, and he appropriately introduced the poem "The Pasture." He then discussed some of his early problems, such as school life, how he didn't like some of his college courses, how he was kicked out, and then chose to become a poet. The children enjoyed the rebellion of Robert Frost.

Mr. Frost and his love of New England were with us during that assembly period, and some of the students could actually picture the scene about the colt as Mr. Frost read:

I think the little fellow's afraid of the snow.
He isn't winter broken. It isn't play
With the little fellow at all. He's running away. . . .

Robert Frost with his deep voice, bushy white hair, and his thoughts and words certainly made an impression.

Mr. Sandburg was next. He made us laugh and then he made us feel sad. It's good to laugh, and it's also good for elementary school children to feel sad, to think, and to express thoughts about being sad. When Mr. Sandburg finished though, the children felt good again.

Langston Hughes was last on the program. He had many funny things to say such as:

> Old Dog Queenie
> Was such a meanie,
> She spent her life
> Barking at the scenery

and

> My mama told me,
> Kindly please,
> Do not get down
> On your knees
> With your brand new
> Clothes on.
> I said, Mom,
> I'm already down.
> Can't I stay
> On the ground
> With my brand new
> Clothes on?
> My mother said,
> No I say!
> So my mother had her way —
> That's why I'm so clean today
> With my brand new
> Clothes on.

The students understood the poet's humor. He made many funny statements, but he also had a very serious message to deliver about the desire for freedom for his race. Quiet engulfed the auditorium as Mr. Hughes read:

> At night when everything is quiet
> This old house seems to breathe a sigh.
> Sometimes I hear a neighbor snoring,
> Sometimes I hear a baby cry,
> Sometimes I hear a staircase creaking,
> Sometimes a distant telephone.
> Then the quiet settles down again,
> The house and I are all alone.
> Lonely house! Lonely me!
> Funny with so many neighbors
> How lonely it can be.
> Oh, lonely street! Lonely town!
> Funny you can be so lonely
> With all these folks around.
> I guess there must be something
> I don't comprehend —
> Sparrows have companions,
> Even stray dogs find a friend.
> The night for me is not romantic.
> Unhook the stars and take them down.
> I'm lonely in this little house
> In this lonely town.

The quiet spell lasted after Mr. Hughes finished reading his poem, for much thought was going on — thoughts about being lonely, lonely because you're black or different, lonely because you're not wanted in a club, thoughts about how mean other children can be. Yes, there were deep thoughts in that auditorium that afternoon.

Then Mr. Hughes startled us with the following words:

Where is the Jim Crow section
On this merry-go-round,
Mister, 'cause I want to ride?
Down South where I come from
White and colored
Can't sit side by side.
Down South on the train
There's a Jim Crow car.
On the bus we're put in the back —
But there ain't no back
To a merry-go-round!
Where's the horse
For a kid that's black?

The children were startled, for the word "black" almost seemed like a dirty word, a word some of them used in anger or to be mean, but here was a Negro poet in front of an audience using the word "black." Some of the students glanced furtively at Harold, a Negro student, and thought of the phrase, "Where's the horse for the kid that's black?"

Mr. Hughes awakened us from our thoughts with stirring words, as if to give us another chance:

I, too, sing America.

I am the darker brother.
They send me to eat in the kitchen
When company comes,
But I laugh,
And eat well,
And grow strong.

Tomorrow,
I'll sit at the table
When company comes.
Nobody'll dare
Say to me,

"Eat in the kitchen,"
Then.

Besides,
They'll see how beautiful I am
And be ashamed.

I, too, am America!

Some of the students felt thrilled that the underdog might some day find his place — his rightful place — in America. I glanced at Harold, and he looked proud!

The audience loved the three poets, but then the recital was over and it was time to return to our classrooms. Deep down in their hearts the audience knew that the three poets weren't really Robert Frost, Carl Sandburg, and Langston Hughes, but John, David, and Doug of the sixth grade. Even deeper in their hearts, however, they knew the spirits of these poets had been present and that they had been touched by their greatness.

Later that week Cynthia, a sixth-grader, volunteered to learn the poem "Mathilda" by the English poet Hilaire Belloc. She was very funny as she impersonated Mathilda, for "Mathilda" is about a little girl who told lies. Our phrase in the poem stresses that Mathilda is a liar, and it was great fun for the class to shout in their loudest voices, "Little Liar." What a wonderful feeling to yell "Little Liar" — it's such a strong expression.

Then someone else presented another Belloc character, "Godolphin Horne who was nobly born." Another student introduced "Rebecca, whom everyone abhors for always slamming doors." Still another child acted out the role of "Henry King, who was always chewing little bits of string." These Hilaire Belloc characters stayed with us all year long, for we seemed to really know them. Our class consisted of twenty-five students plus Rebecca Offendort, Henry King, Godolphin Horne, and last, but not least, Mathilda!

Other words and thoughts placed in the Poetry Pot included the strange life of Emily Dickinson and how one day she went to her upstairs room and stayed there the rest of her life as a recluse looking out on the world through her window. Some of the children laughed at first, but as Miss Dickinson's spirit permeated the classroom, they stopped laughing and started listening to her very personal, sensitive thoughts.

Poetry can be many things, and sometimes it is a man or a woman sharing his soul with students, trusting them to share his soul, trusting them enough to relate his most personal thoughts, trusting them enough to know they won't laugh. Nobody laughed at Miss Emily, as we fondly called her, after we came to know her. Miss Emily's words were words one didn't forget, for they formed a clear, concise picture in one's mind:

> I'll tell you how the sun rose, —
> A ribbon at a time . . .

and

> The robin is the one
> That interrupts the morn . . .

and

> The sky is low, the clouds are mean . . .

Some of the children will never forget Miss Emily at her window. She wrote a letter to the world that never answered back, but the nine-, ten-, and eleven-year-olds who felt the spirit of Emily Dickinson responded with great sympathy to her words. They seemed to understand the gentle thoughts of this woman. So many times school children have looked at the world though their windows, particularly classroom windows with a teacher's voice droning away in the distance.

One day as the Poetry Pot smoldered, the strains of a guitar were heard. The guitar played on and on, and the class was not quite sure how to react. I introduced the poem "The Lament of the Guitar." Lament was a new word that helped the class enter another new world, the world of Federico Garcia Lorca, the Spanish poet. The children sensed the hypnotic trance of a sad Spanish guitar, and then they truly knew the feeling of a lament.

Then hoof beats sounded in the distance:

> Córdoba.
> Far away and alone.
>
> Black pony, big moon,
> and olives in my saddle-bag.
> Although I know the roads
> I'll never reach Córdoba. . . .
>
> Ay! How long the road!
> Ay! My valiant pony!
> Ay! That death should wait me
> before I reach Córdoba.
>
> Córdoba.
> Far away and alone.

I introduced creative dancing to seven- and eight-year-olds as a boy volunteered to be the horse on the way to Córdoba. The room was very still as he slowly moved his legs like a horse, shook his mane, and began his trip. There was one steady beat after another as his shoes hit the classroom floor. Then every single child in that room attempted to make the trip to Córdoba. Their hoofbeats were strong but sad, sounds just as Senor Lorca would have wanted.

We moved on to the city of Seville. Bullfight sounds echoed through this old Spanish city; there were screams of "Ole! Ole!" Perhaps the greatest poem of all time about a bullfighter is "The Death of Ignacio Sanchez Mejias":

> The wounds were burning like suns
> *at five in the afternoon,*
> and the crowd was breaking the windows
> *at five in the afternoon.*
> At five in the afternoon.
> Ah, that fatal five in the afternoon!
> It was five by all the clocks!
> It was five in the shade of the afternoon! . . .

With these words the students sensed the admiration and love Lorca felt for his friend the bullfighter:

> It will be a long time, if ever, before there is born
> an Andalusian so true, so rich in adventure.
> I sing of his elegance with words that groan,
> and I remember a sad breeze through the olive
> trees. . . .

With Lorca's words and thoughts in their minds, none of the students ever need to go to Spain to understand his love of his country or ever need attend a bullfight to sense the excitement and tragedy of the arena. Elementary school children are receptive to the sadness of Lorca, but they need a teacher who will allow Senor Lorca to enter the room.

During one assembly period one hundred ten fifth- and sixth-graders sat on a pitch-black stage in a pitch-black auditorium and presented "The Congo" by Vachel Lindsay. It was an overpowering, overwhelming experience as the violence of "The Congo" bounced from wall to wall. The audience and the cast loved the blackness, loved the strange rhythms, and loved the whispering, but most of all they loved the screams of blood! As the poem unfolded through choral speech plus some solo lines, the pulse beat became more tense. The drums played by some of the boys began to be heard. Three boys and three girls had volunteered to do some impromptu dancing, and with just a suggestion of indirect lighting, the audience could see grotesque shadows wavering on the walls. As the poem drew to a close, the one hundred ten voices faded, became barely audible, and slowed down to a snail's pace with the final line, "Mumbo . . . jumbo . . . will . . . hoo . . . doo . . . you!"

It took great teamwork on the children's part to sense each other's rhythm and to remain in unison. The one hundred ten creators held the final "you-u-u-u-u" until they ran out of breath. And then, after a long, long pause during which the audience waited, not quite sure whether the poem was over or not, the one hundred ten let out the most barbaric, blood-curdling scream in the history of elementary education! Then the auditorium lights flashed on. For weeks the younger children buzzed about that final scream.

Certainly it was difficult to arrange the poem into a dramatic form in which so many students could participate. It was hard, like walking though the Congo itself, but we made it. We made it because the students wanted to succeed, wanted to accept the challenge of new words and thoughts, and wanted to understand and know another poet.

One day in the classroom Rush, a sixth-grader, impersonated the East Indian poet Rabindranath Tagore. Softly and gently he read some of Tagore's stories about children, about paper boats, and the wicked postman. Rabindranath Tagore told the class many things before he left. He told us such things as, "The sparrow is sorry for the peacock at the burden of its tail," and "Wrong cannot afford defeat, but Right can." The students were glad they had an opportunity to meet Tagore in their school.

The Poetry Pot bubbled all year long. The children were exposed to the Chinese poet Ai Ching, Tennyson, Whitman, and many others. The fire under the Poetry Pot never died out. A wisp of smoke rose when we least expected it, and it was pleasant to be surprised by a visit from a poet or poetess.

There was no specific time of the day or week when the Poetry Pot boiled; there was no scheduled poetry period. Sometimes I, as the teacher, was in the mood to present a poet, or some mornings someone in the class would arrive eager to introduce a poet. One cannot schedule the mood of poets.

Never once did our Poetry Pot bubble alliteration, onomatopoeia, or metaphor. We were interested in the thoughts of the poets and in attempting to enter their world. Reading should be a love of thoughts, a love of people, and a medium for dreaming, even if one doesn't understand it all.

There is always time in any elementary school for a

chat with a poet. There is always time in the curriculum for a touch of greatness.

I won't easily forget the dancing in the dark when we dramatized Vachel Lindsay's "The Congo" or the sirens and red lights of his "The Firemen's Ball." I never knew poetry could be so interesting. You gave me a taste of literature and the arts I will never forget. And for non-believers who say that fifth- and sixth-graders don't need and understand good literature, Mr. Cullum certainly did me a favor with an early introduction to literature.

Priscilla Frank, 1965

I definitely developed an interest in poetry which has continued; in fact, I now keep a "book" of my favorite poems all typed on separate sheets.

Nancy Terhune, 1957

The poetry recitations made little effect on me until I realized what poetry was. I usually just prepared poems to recite only, even if I didn't understand them, but an incident in class changed that. I prepared a poem by Longfellow which I did not understand at all, and you realized this. After I began, you asked whether I understood the poem or not. I was stunned when you told me to understand a poem before reciting it. From then on, I began to interpret everything I read.

Jim Hadley, 1960

Being in "John Brown's Body" was one of the most enriching and meaningful experiences of my life. Performing great literature, unlike reading it, is living intimately with it, working under its spell, and gaining a lasting impression of its thrilling and immediate beauty. Something in the poem got to me, somehow, and I will never let it go.

Laura Webber, 1965

From Sea to Shining Sea

A LARGE BLUE SHOWER CURTAIN spread on the floor represented the Atlantic Ocean as ten first-graders were the first to dare to plunge in. Some were hesitant to begin swimming, but soon the excitement of dodging make-believe waves encouraged everyone to swim. It was a crowded Atlantic Ocean in that Midland School first grade; however, each of the thirty-one students managed to get at least one foot wet.

Jumping into the Atlantic Ocean was the beginning of my cross-country trip with my thirty-one first-graders with the permission of their well-adjusted homeroom teacher. Without her cooperation we would not have made too much progress across this fantastic country of ours. Whenever I had a free fifteen minutes or so, I would visit Mrs. Corradi's class, usually twice a week.

As the language arts teacher of the Rye Public School System I felt that the ideal way to learn almost anything is through creative play. So why not a little geography?

I did not need permission slips from parents for the trip for we never left the classroom, yet we traveled far and wide on all kinds of conveyances.

After everyone had dried off from his ocean dip we were ready for the trip to the big city of New York, which is not far from the wet Atlantic Ocean. The large blue shower curtain was neatly folded by three or four six-year-old helpers—well, almost neatly folded—and we started our twenty-five-mile hike to New York City.

How did we establish a feeling of New York City? We spread a large piece of brown wrapping paper on the floor, and almost everyone helped create the fabulous city of millions by drawing window after window after window. Bunny claimed she drew hundreds and hundreds of windows; Brett said thirty, and Chris said he didn't know but his hand was tired of drawing blue, black, and red windows.

The resulting mural had a delicate Paul Klee strength. How we admired our array of windows depicting a city where some of their fathers worked. It was a busy, busy city, even if our mural contained only windows with imaginary faces pressed against the window panes.

As the windows were being rolled up and put away, alligators rushed to a corner of the room, nearly knocking each other down while finding a comfortable sleeping position in Okeefenokee Swamp. It was a hot, damp, humid swamp, but the thirty-one alligators didn't seem to mind. Occasionally I would hear a voice saying, "Mr. Cullum, Paul is crushing me!" Most of the time there were squeals of delight at being piled on top of one another.

The alligators dozed and basked in the noonday sun, contented as could be, when I "accidentally" stepped into Okeefenokee Swamp. The thirty-one alligators slowly raised their heads, looked about, and then slowly but surely headed in my direction displaying stern disapproval. Yes, they attacked the intruder as any self-respecting alligator would do.

One alligator was so belligerent he punched me on the head. I think it was Eddie, but I have no proof. I was very fortunate to escape from Okeefenokee Swamp alive and with only a slight tear in my sports jacket. The swamp soon dried up, and the thirty-one alligators returned to their seats.

Many hands next volunteered to swim down the long Mississippi River. What was the Mississippi River? It was another long piece of brown paper that stretched the length of the room when all the desks were pushed back. The children took off their shoes and socks so as not to tear the paper while they were swimming. It was tiring swimming down Old Man River, and some gave up and began to crawl down the river.

While some of the children were still attempting to reach the Delta, the rest of the class sang:

> He just keeps rollin'
> He just keeps rollin'
> He just keeps rollin'
> He just keeps rollin'
> He just keeps rollin'

One day we came close to singing that phrase one hundred times. I believe it was Debbie who ran out of breath doing all that singing and exclaimed, "It sure is a long river, Mr. Cullum!"

When everyone had completed the arduous task of swimming down the river, the Mississippi was rolled up and put away. We were then approximately halfway across the country.

What would we encounter next? Why, Pikes Peak, of course. Slowly, but surely and steadily, about six of us started building Pikes Peak. The rest of the class watched with avid interest as Pikes Peak grew taller and taller. Mrs. Corradi was a trifle nervous about our building a mountain, but we reassured her that if Pikes Peak collapsed, it would collapse in the right direction.

It was not easy building the peak for the little folding chairs were difficult to balance. Tension built up in that first-grade classroom as Pikes Peak became higher and higher.

"Where are we heading, boys and girls?"

"Pikes Peak or Bust!" was the response.

Pikes Peak slowly began to lean in the right direction with a gentle push from me. Those first-grade eyes were big as the peak slowly began its downward plunge. Frank held his ears just before the crash, and they all screamed "PIKES PEAK OR BUST!" Mrs. Corradi was relieved when our visit to Pikes Peak was over, and we returned the chairs to their proper places.

Just before we headed for the Rocky Mountains, Diane spoke to me privately, "Mr. Cullum, my mother doesn't think I should take such a dangerous trip as to climb up the Rockies!"

"I agree with your mother, Diane, but would it be all right if it were a make-believe trip?"

"Yes, make-believe trips are all right, but I still might change my mind."

When the class was ready to have an adventure in the wild Rockies, I asked them to place their heads on their desks and to cover their eyes. As they obeyed my request, I quickly slipped into the bear suit I had rented for the occasion.

When they opened their eyes and saw a huge grizzly confronting them, their reaction was a spontaneous gasp of awe and excitement. Was it really a grizzly or was it Mr. Cullum? Brett started dancing on his toes at the mere thought of meeting a grizzly, real or make-believe!

Some were uncertain and slightly hesitant, but before the day was over everyone had become quite friendly with Mr. Grizzly of the Rocky Mountains. Even Mrs. Corradi was reassured, for that particular grizzly hugged her and planted a wet kiss on her cheek in appreciation for allowing all this creative play in the first grade with a dash of geographical concepts thrown in.

Soon I removed the grizzly head, and everyone had a chance to try it on. Evie did a delightful dance while wearing the head.

Even though one young lady kept calling the Rocky Mountains Bumpy Hill, the trip was successful. Even Diane no longer seemed concerned about the danger. What were the Rocky Mountains? Simply the classroom plus a little bit of imagination and, of course, a real live grizzly.

I was delighted to climb out of that bear suit for it was very warm. Speaking of warm, the class next prepared for an experience with a hot desert sun. Oh, the power of that burning sun!

WATER! Everyone wanted and needed water! To simulate desert conditions, we closed all the windows on a hot June day as the children gathered around the water fountain to fill their canteens for the treacherous trip through the Mojave Desert. Not everyone had a canteen, but all did have some sort of container — most had soda bottles. They knew the importance of having plenty of water as we prepared to cross the desert.

The room became quite warm, and some of the boys took off their shirts and T-shirts. I think it was Paul who mentioned the foolishness of exposing one's skin to a hot desert sun, but his scientific thinking did not make too much of an impression. The travelers felt comfortable and secure as long as they had plenty of wet water with them. They never once gulped their water for they knew the value of this precious liquid. They knew they had to ration it, so they took only one gulp every few miles and let the water slowly trickle down their throats. One young lady claimed she drank two gallons before we completed the desert trip. Perhaps she miscalculated slightly, but everyone had to go to the bathroom as soon as we left the desert. No one suffered from heat stroke, but it was refreshing to open the windows.

Our trip was nearly over because directly in front of us at the back of the room was the Pacific Ocean. This time we used a large blue shower curtain with a rip in it so we could tell the difference between the two oceans. As they held their noses, jumping in the Pacific Ocean was just as much fun as swimming in the Atlantic.

"Well, boys and girls, it's time to head back to Westchester County, New York, so let's dry off and get started because it's nearly time for lunch."

How did we manage to recross our vast country so quickly? That was easy. All we did was push all the desks together to form one large mass of land, and we slowly walked across the desks. Now the children knew there was an enormous piece of land between the Atlantic and Pacific Oceans.

Our canteens were ready, so off we started. Back through the Mojave Desert, over the Rockies, right by Pikes Peak, down the Mississippi River, through Okeefenokee Swamp, past the hundreds of windows of New York City, and home at last near the Atlantic Ocean in dear old Rye.

Of course, we missed some vital areas such as the Great Plains and the Great Lakes, but children can learn about those in the second grade. Crossing the country with thirty-one first-graders is a delightful experience. It's worth experiencing at least once!

I Recall being the alagators and The Mississippi river. And the waves. And when we made mountains and the noise it made was very loud. And when we walked across the Atlantic ocean and Pacific. All were fun. And come and see us on my birthday.

Bunny Birrell, 1966

We crossed the Okefenokee Swamp. We crossed the pacific and atlantic ocean. We flew across the United States in a plain and on motor sickles. Once you snuck in with your bear custum.

Brett Pierce, 1966

It was all real fun. I liked when we swam in the pacific ocean and nobody wanted to come back. I liked the bear suit because it made you feel you were in a real woods.

Frank Anfuso, 1966

A Grammar Hospital

HOW IS YOUR SENTENCE SENSE? Is a fragment of your sentence slipping? Did you apply the comma correctly? Be careful, you're stepping on a dangling modifier!

The eight ways in which words are used are called the eight parts of speech. The eight classifications are:

NOUN — a noun expresses action or a state of being.

PRONOUN — a pronoun takes the place of something.

VERB — a very strong feeling.

ADJECTIVE — shows extra strong feeling.

ADVERB — an adverb modifies a noun, pronoun, adjective, adverb, preposition, conjunction, and I think an interjection.

PREPOSITION — a preposition most of the time is a tiny word.

CONJUNCTION — a conjunction connects nouns and nouns, and if you don't have a noun, use a pronoun that can take the place of anything.

INTERJECTION — shows extra, extra strong feeling.

These definitions of the eight parts of speech, of course, are *incorrect*, but these are the definitions I received when I asked for them from nine-, ten-, and eleven-year-olds the day after a parts-of-speech exam in which they had received perfect scores.

Traditional grammar lingo in the elementary schools is "for the birds!" There is no reality to it, the concept of parts of speech is too abstract for students to grasp, and it is also a big bore! But being a public servant and at the bottom of the ladder, I was required to teach grammar and the parts of speech. For years I had been saying, "A noun is the name of a person, place, or thing, and a proper noun is the name of a specific person, place, or thing."

One season I could not face another year of monotony, another year of looking at the dullness in the children's eyes and feeling the dullness in my soul, simply to satisfy the junior high school staff, my principal, and the tax payers. In desperation I opened the Elementary School Grammar Hospital. I was ready with my blood-stained medical gown and twenty-five surgical masks ready to hand out to my interns.

As the Grammar Hospital opened, I explained to the class that this year we were going to operate on all the parts of speech to see if we could stop the "bleeding." They would pretend they were interns in a hospital, and the first patients would be nouns. We would review nouns until we were exhausted, and then days later we would put on our surgical masks to see if we could operate successfully on the noun patients. If the class average was below 80, then we would continue studying nouns.

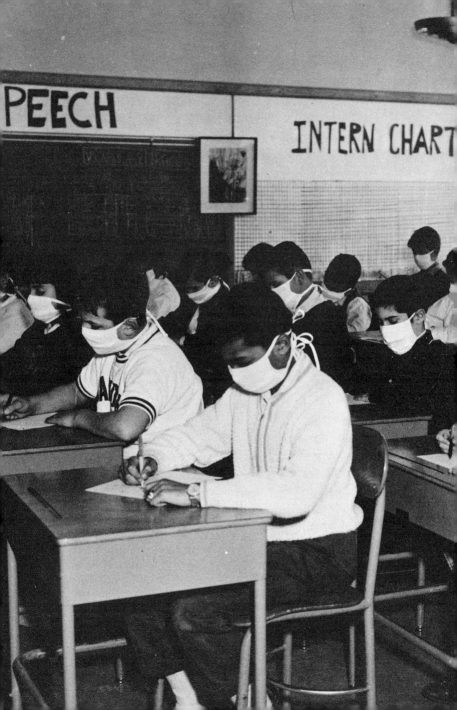

Carefully and in the technically correct manner, students put on their surgical masks, ready for the noun patients to be wheeled into the room.

The "medical" tests I gave the children were quite challenging, but fair. For example, to test nouns I prepared twenty sentences in which the students had to circle the common nouns and underline the proper nouns. Each sentence had to be completely correct for any credit. I had four sixth-grade classes for English, and each wanted to be first to operate successfully on the eight parts of speech.

It began to be exciting. I encouraged the students to ask all types of questions, no matter how ridiculous or how absurd, and the classes began to relax.

"I understand what you're saying, Mr. Cullum, I understand the words, but prepositions don't make sense," declared Bert.

"That state of being verb sure is tricky and weird," remarked Eleanor.

Now the students were beginning to be honest about their insecurity in this area, and this uneasiness served as a common ground — a common ground of helping one another, a common ground of not being afraid to admit they didn't understand something, even though we had been working on that part of speech for two days.

Visiting consultants helped the class. Who were these consultants? They were simply students in the class who assumed my role as the teacher and explained to their peers how they approached a grammatical problem. Sometimes their direct, simple explanations were far superior to mine.

I could feel the sense of relaxation spreading; doubts about parts of speech began to disappear, because the tension of having to understand parts of speech disappeared. Often a particularly slow intern asked for special help from his fellow interns, and in a corner of the room or in the hallway five-minute briefing sessions were held. This in turn developed into great team play.

One sixth-grade class blackboard chart looked like this:

PATIENTS	CLASS AVERAGE	
Nouns	91	
Pronouns	90	
Verbs	88	
Adverbs	71	(here we are still operating)
Adjectives	80	(just did make it)
Prepositions	62	(patient bleeding badly)
Conjunctions	97	(much rejoicing)
Interjections	92	

By the end of the school year we had solved the problem of the neurotic adverb and the constipated preposition. My interns graduated to the junior high school as full-fledged doctors specializing in the field of parts of speech. Today is the age of specialization, so we were right in step with the times. The following school year the junior high school reported that those Grammar Hospital graduates really knew their grammar and parts of speech.

Why was the Grammar Hospital successful? It was successful because those eleven-year-olds sensed a touch of greatness in the medical profession . . . that's all, it was that simple. The greatness did not stem from the parts of speech but from putting on a surgical mask, from the challenge of the quizzes, and from the feeling of success when the class reached an average of at least 80. This school magic should exist in all elementary schools, public or private.

This magical excitement is what kindergartners through six-graders seek, and they will continue to seek it until they find it in the school world, outside the school world, or in their daydreams. Because the children became emotionally involved with the parts of speech, they remembered the dreary details of what a noun is or what an adverb modifies.

Some of the more advanced interns did some fantastically creative drawings of a Mrs. Noun before and after her visit to the Grammar Hospital, of a Jack Preposition before and after, and of many other characters. They were comical stick figures that we posted in the hallway so the children of other grades could see the progress a particular favorite of theirs was making.

It was fun for the students to be interns, it was fun wearing the surgical masks, and more than likely it will probably be the only opportunity I will have to be the major-domo of a full-fledged hospital. Saving the lives of the parts of speech saved my sanity that particular school year.

Everyone hates grammar, but you made a game out of it, and I even enjoyed learning grammar.

Barbara Zelner, 1963

Eventually grammar came naturally, and we were able to combine a creative piece of writing with correct grammar and punctuation.

Louise Lipman, 1963

Dry Ice Hockey

IT SEEMS A SHAME TO STAY in a stale, cluttered classroom or a smelly gymnasium for a play period when outside the wind is howling, the snow is flying, and there is a tempestuous quality in the air. Emotions are very much a part of elementary school life, and no matter how hard teachers try, we cannot separate the excitement of the outside winter world from the dreams of students in the health-controlled temperatures of the safe classrooms.

The Dry Ice Hockey League was organized during the winter of 1948 at St. Luke's School in Greenwich Village. It consisted of my fourth-grade boys who played during their after-lunch play period on a small asphalt playground that had no ice. There were no skates either, but each boy had an ice-hockey stick he had purchased for the game. Two fairly large wooden boxes that several of the boys had discovered in the neighborhood served as goalie cages. Instead of a real hockey puck, I furnished a roll of black friction tape that wouldn't hurt if it struck a youngster. My nine-year-old friends provided the vivid imagination that created a hockey rink in the school yard.

What excitement was generated on that asphalt! Everyone experienced the sensation and excitement of actually skating, and when a goal was about to be scored, the energy and enthusiasm equaled that of a Stanley Cup Playoff at Madison Square Garden. The lightning reflexes of Bobby and Harry, the leadership of Mark and Kit, and the exuberance of Barry flashing his hockey stick like a Shakespearean foil were a delight to behold.

All the St. Luke's boys became involved both physically and emotionally. The program expanded until it included all the boys from the fourth through eighth grades. Everyone played. In fact one young lady of fourth-grade vintage joined in, and she was good! Sometimes she was even better than some of the boys. Why shouldn't girls play hockey too?

Everyone played and felt comfortably successful because they were not judged on their athletic prowess nor on their ability to display good sportsmanship or to become part of the group. All the boys were asked to do was to put on their imaginary skates and skate as fast as they could on the imaginary ice.

When the playground was partially covered with snow and real ice, there were many belly laughs over some very realistic tumbles. Sometimes the growth and development of a twenty-minute play period seem so significant that I felt no guilt in allowing it to continue beyond the scheduled stopping point. Early in my teaching career I discovered that the ideal place to study and observe children is on the playground. And the playground is perhaps the easiest place to join them.

The St. Luke's School I knew from 1948 to 1956 was a school of charm and enchantment, for it contained no specialists. We teachers ate with the students, played with them, studied with them, learned with them, painted with them, sang with them, and most of all day-dreamed with them. There were tremendous daydreams on that asphalt as boys "skated" up and down the "ice." The desire to win was strong, but the comradeship was even stronger.

Often impromptu after-school games started that in-volved students, teachers, and clergy. I still remember scoring an occasional goal with much huffing and puffing, Mr. Moore, the tall sexton of St. Luke's Chapel, being whacked accidentally by a sixth-grader's stick, and Father Moore and Father Leach giving the faculty team a helping hand. When the final score was announced, however, it always seemed to be: Students: 17, Faculty: 16.

When I changed from private school life to public school life, the dry ice hockey game went right along with me. From 1956 to 1966 there were also great moments of living on the asphalt playground of the Mid-land School.

My main function was to establish the structure for the Dry Ice Hockey League. The League consisted of two teams, the Rangers and the Blackhawks. We tried to make the teams as evenly balanced as possible each year. Two co-captains for each team were appointed by me, and I assumed the role of referee — and only that role.

The co-captains directed their respective teams and were responsible for settling arguments, breaking up fights, handling substitutions, planning strategy, boosting morale, lecturing indifferent players, congratulating a great defensive play, and so on. Many times the decisions of the co-captains were not wise ones, but they learned through experience.

We kept interesting, detailed records that were published monthly in the school paper, *The Chatterbox*. Here is a sample report:

MIDLAND SCHOOL HOCKEY SEASON

****
* MIDLAND RANGERS WIN
1961–1962 HOCKEY CHAMPIONSHIP *

****
Final Scoring Statistics

		Goals	Assists	Points
1.	Wallace Terhune	39	24	63
2.	Chris Ley	34	22	56
3.	T. Pickering	35	20	55
4.	Cam Gerrish	22	33	55
5.	John Anderson	9	41	50
6.	Andy Benson	18	29	47
7.	Teddy Haley	17	30	47
8.	Carl Bernsten	20	25	45
9.	Ken Ramirez	22	20	42
10.	Jim Pugh	12	28	40
11.	Ronnie Dunn	16	17	33
12.	Terry Rankin	12	13	25
13.	Paul Julius	8	12	20
14.	Jim Briganti	10	8	18
15.	Joe Guglielmo	5	6	11

MIDLAND SCHOOL IS PROUD OF BOTH RANGERS AND BLACKHAWKS!
THE SPORTSMANSHIP WAS WONDERFUL ! ! ! ! ! ! ! ! ! ! ! !

It was the boys' hockey league. There was love, violence, danger, and success on that dry ice hockey field — all the things elementary school children so desperately need. I remember boys scoring the first goal of their non-athletic lives and tears of joy streaming down their cheeks. I will never forget the moments when some of those boys realized for the first time that they belonged — they were accepted by their peers and were pounded on the back by those whom they had admired but never thought would accept them.

As the years progressed, the teams were better equipped with sturdy masks, better goalie cages, and shin guards, but the basis of the game remained the same. Neither snow, nor sleet, nor rain could stop our dry ice hockey sorties three times a week and frequently on Saturdays. The adult world had difficulty understanding that rain didn't really wet us nor snow really make us feel cold.

What basic skills were stressed? None! All I did was give the youngsters an opportunity to score a goal, to rub shoulders with other boys, and to feel important, even if just for a fleeting second.

Dry ice hockey is perhaps the aspect of school life I miss the most, for without realizing it, the children revealed themselves in creative situations with intense pride and an energy full of positive thinking. Two teams opposed each other, but actually one large family group exercised its creative force.

Many boys . . . many memories. I can still see Paul splashing in a muddy puddle as he stopped a goal from being scored, Jim and his tiny hockey stick, the fine sportsmanship of Campbell when he allowed the winning goal to slip by him in an overtime championship game, Andy's drive, Bryson, Larry, and Corky "skating" down the asphalt ice as they charged the opposing goalie, David, scoring champion of all time with 185 points, the day Bill developed blisters from his new shoes, and the protective feeling the sixth-grade boys showed for the younger players of the second and third grades.

I feel fortunate having shared so many moments of dry ice hockey with hundreds of elementary school boys — moments of no ice and no skates — but many, many, moments of greatness.

I will never forget how you got me interested in hockey for if it wasn't for you I would never have started playing.

Andy Benson, 1964

One of my favorite activities was the after-school hockey program. Though I was reluctant at first, I'm glad you persuaded me to join. I can remember the date of my first goal . . . January 19, 1959.

Laird Myers, 1959

I would say that besides having fun in your class, the after-school hockey program was better. In the hockey games there was not only the tension of playing the game, but also the pure fun we had. There was also the thrill you had when most people would be inside watching the rain, snow, or sleet come down, but there would be twenty-five kids from second grade to sixth grade playing hockey.

Eric Silver, 1966

Because of my introduction to hockey, I took a plane trip to Canada where I stayed at a hockey camp for part of the summer. My real feelings toward you is not as a teacher, but as a good guy whom I could talk to and confide in.

Scott Young, 1965

My fondest memory is the hockey program. The three games a week never lost their interest. I still have the school newspaper listing the standings and the scores for all the boys. One of the high points of the year was going as a group to Madison Square Garden to see the N.Y. Rangers play.

Martin Seim, 1961

The Longfellow Lab

WHEN I WAS A LANGUAGE ARTS teacher in the
Rye Public School System, I was lucky to be working for
and with Superintendent Dr. Joseph Grimes, Jr. He was
a man who could balance a budget and yet always had
time to sit down with his teachers to daydream about
the endless possibilities for excitement that a school system could generate between the hours nine to three. We
did not envision a three-ring circus but rather creating
an atmosphere for stepping into the unknown and add-
ing new dimensions to the lives of students.

Sometimes those daydream discussions became a reality, such as when he permitted me to disregard the reading workbooks and basal texts and gave me the money
to purchase the complete works of Longfellow for each
sixth-grader in the school system, a total of one hundred and one students. He gave me permission to de-
part from the established reading curriculum, for we
both knew in our hearts that sixth-graders are ready for
Hiawatha, the first American superman; we knew that

today's eleven-year-olds are ready for Evangeline's long search; we knew that the kids are ready for the challenge of grown-up reading; but most of all we knew with Longfellow that:

> A boy's will is the wind's will,
> And the thoughts of youth are long, long thoughts. . . .

The ten- and eleven-year-olds of today want strong, sound literature; they want to read writers whose ideas they can attack and defend.

I was excited the first week I introduced the complete works of Longfellow to my four sixth-grade classes of English. The book I used was *The Poems of Longfellow*, a Modern Library Book published by Random House. Some students gulped, others gasped, others nearly cheered when they realized that reading workbooks were now ancient history!

The rhythm of "Hiawatha" fascinated us, and after laughing at the phrase:

> By the shores of Gitche Gumee,
> By the shining Big-Sea-Water, . . .

we became very involved with the gallant warrior and his sweetheart, Minnehaha. The excitement of Hiawatha overcoming his obstacles engrossed all of us.

Of course there were academic rough spots, but I, the English teacher, was there. That's what I was paid for — to help students overcome some of the difficulties. I anticipated instilling in the students the confidence to attempt challenging literature, to feel comfortable reading poetry, and to accept strange vocabulary. At first I did all the reading, but within a week *they* wanted to read the Longfellow rhythms out loud, and I was more than willing to allow them to take over. I think it was Ann or Sherry who asked, "Why can't we read instead of you?"

This broke the ice, and soon many hands were volunteering to read page after page. Every chapter held their interest. There were moments of silence and awe when we read about Hiawatha's childhood:

> Then upon one knee uprising,
> Hiawatha aimed an arrow;
> Scarce a twig moved with his motion,
> Scarce a leaf was stirred or rustled,
> But the wary roebuck started,
> Stamped with all his hoofs together,
> Listened with one foot uplifted,
> Leaped as if to meet the arrow;
> Ah! the singing, fatal arrow,
> Like a wasp it buzzed and stung him!

What quiet tension vibrated through the room. Each sixth grade reacted in exactly the same manner — like a wasp it stung *them!* We stopped to discuss this Longfellow portrait in words, words that leaped and challenged the creative emotions of the students. There were no yawns and no looking out the window to watch a third-grade group playing on the soccer field. Mr. Longfellow's greatness had touched us all!

There were many such moments:

> Go not forth O Hiawatha!
> To the kingdom of the West-Wind,
> To the realms of Mudjekeewis,
> Lest he harm you with his magic
> Lest he kill you with his cunning!

Hiawatha ignored Nokomis, his grandmother, and the children fought along with him in every major and minor encounter. I still feel the thrill of the classes' interest in the description of Hiawatha on his way to kill Pearl Feather:

> All the air was white with moonlight,
> All the water black with shadow,
> And around him the Suggema,
> The mosquito, sang his war song,
> And the fireflies, Wah-wah-taysee,
> Waved their torches to mislead him;
> And the bullfrog, the Dahinda,
> Thrust his head into the moonlight,
> Fixed his yellow eyes upon him,
> Sobbed and sank beneath the surface;
> And anon a thousand whistles,
> Answered over all the fenlands,
> And the heron, the Shuh-shuh-gah,
> Far off on the reedy margin,
> Heralded the hero's coming.

As I observed the classes, I remembered vividly elementary school students complaining about books that had too much description, but here were four sixthgrade classes spellbound by description. There were many such moments in the twenty-two chapters, but the last chapter, "Hiawatha's Departure," contained the climax, and no doubt that's the way it should be:

> And the forests, dark and lonely,
> Moved through all their depths of darkness,
> Sighed, "Farewell, O Hiawatha!"
> And the waves upon the margin
> Rising, rippling on the pebbles,
> Sobbed, "Farewell, O Hiawatha!"
> And the heron, the Shuh-shuh-gah,
> From her haunts among the fenlands,
> Screamed, "Farewell, O Hiawatha!"

Thus departed Hiawatha!
Hiawatha the Beloved,
In the glory of the sunset,
In the purple mists of evening,
To the regions of the home-wind,
Of the Northwest Wind, Keewaydin,
To the islands of the Blessed,
To the Kingdom of Ponemah,
To the land of the Hereafter!

Many eyes were moist; I know mine were partly because of Longfellow's poetic gifts and partly because of one hundred and one students who had confirmed my opinion that they had the ability and nobility to accept a touch of greatness. Their silence at the end of the poem as Hiawatha vanished into the heavens told me that school life need not be routine, dull, or one long series of learning basic skills. We teachers must reach the hearts of children before they are impressed with our basic skills.

Some of the students dusted off the Longfellow volumes they found on their family bookshelves and reread "Hiawatha" on their own.

The Longfellow Lab next tackled another Longfellow epic, "Evangeline." This is a love story, and often some educators will automatically state that eleven-year-olds will not accept a love poem — it will cause laughter and derision. True, students might laugh at a Gabriel or an Evangeline but not Longfellow's Evangeline. The students who finished studying "Hiawatha" with me would not laugh at any of Longfellow's works, for they had been touched by his genius. The young-at-heart recognized again his touch of greatness from the very opening lines:

> This is the forest primeval.
> The murmuring pines and the hemlocks,
> Bearded with moss . . .

They accepted the gentle mood of the Acadian land that was to be overwhelmed by tragedy. They met Father Felician, Basil, Benedict, and others and felt the same anger they did when the village of Grand Pré was destroyed and Evangeline and Gabriel were separated. Years passed:

> Dear Child, why dream and wait for him longer?
> Are there not other youths as fair as Gabriel?
> Others who have hearts as tender and true, and
> spirits as loyal?

But my one hundred and one sixth-graders knew that Evangeline would search for her Gabriel until she found him. We wandered with Evangeline day after day, and it seemed to me that a haunting melody lingered over the room as the class sensed the tragic love of Evangeline. There was no laughter, no giggling. The haunting melody grew stronger as Evangeline kept just missing Gabriel. Finally she did find him:

> Vainly he strove to rise
> And Evangeline kneeling beside him
> Kissed his dying lips, and laid his head on her bosom.
> Sweet was the light of his eyes, but it suddenly sank
> into darkness,
> As when a lamp is blown out by a gust of wind at a
> casement.

Do you know what those eleven-year-olds discussed at the end of "Evangeline?" They discussed how unfair life can be to some individuals. This is a large concept for young minds and worth discussing. From the discussion came the conclusion that life is not deliberately mean or spiteful and that quite often people must adjust to adversity. These were children of elementary school vintage who concluded that people must adjust — not trained psychiatrists. I was proud of their thinking.

I know my eleven-year-olds will repeat the story of Evangeline to all who will listen, and I know that some will wander up to Acadia to relive the tragic tale and to see if they can find shadows of Longfellow's poem.

In a typical session in the Longfellow Lab, a sixth-grade class entered my room and immediately started reading at the place we had left off the day before. Volunteers read to the class, and at the end of each canto they did not want to rehash the section, they wanted to go on. The fervor of following the life of Hiawatha or the search of Evangeline was with them. Only the sound of the bell disturbed us. The school schedule could not be disrupted, and classes were exchanged. My classes would have been willing to read whole poems at one sitting — and why not!

Next we read the "Courtship of Miles Standish," and it was as easily handled as the first two poems. Then we turn to "Tales of a Wayside Inn," also easily handled.

By April we had completed the works of Longfellow, and the Longfellow Lab was closed for the year — well, not completely closed, for during the Easter vacation a group of students, on a volunteer basis, started a Hiawatha Art Colony. Huge pieces of cardboard, bottles of poster paint, big brushes, and no art teacher's rules helped produce the most glorious murals of Long-fellow's "Hiawatha" that I have ever seen. The murals depicted such scenes as the crows attacking the blessed cornfields, as painted by Carmela, the sea gulls tearing the sturgeon apart so that Hiawatha could escape, as painted by Joanne, and the death of Kwasind as he was struck by pine cones thrown by the evil little people, as painted by Susan.

Speaking of the evil little people, we weren't allowed to paint in the classroom or the hallways because we might dirty the floor, so we dragged everything out-doors. It wasn't the warmest Easter vacation on record, but bundled up, with students hanging on to the huge cardboards so that they wouldn't blow away, the volun-teers completed twelve stunning Hiawatha murals.

After the Easter vacation my sixth-graders visited the primary grades with the huge murals and told the legend of this great Indian to eager attentive audiences of five-, six-, and seven-year-olds. As the murals were carried into a primary grade, one at a time, the "oohs" and "aahs" of the young ones were exhilarating. It will be a long time before they forget the deeds of Hiawatha. Those first-graders might not ever hear the words of Henry Wadsworth Longfellow again in their elemen-tary school lives, but that doesn't make any difference, for they were exposed to and touched by his greatness. All it takes is one gentle touch of genius, and like Cracker Jacks, the more one eats, the more one wants!

At the graduation exercises in June, my sixth-graders presented selections from "Hiawatha" in choral speech form. I looked at my school superintendent, and without saying a word, we both knew that the Longfellow Lab had been a success.

Why shouldn't the creative giants of the world succeed in an elementary school? In our elementary schools sit the creative geniuses of tomorrow, and it's the classroom teacher's job to see that young creative people are exposed to all kinds of experiences and emotions. It's our job to see that they don't give up their dreams too early in their lives.

If you don't like Longfellow, start an Edgar Allan Poe Pantry, or a Walt Whitman Well, but start something where students can forget staying in line, sitting up tall, or praying for a fast three o'clock!

Stop! I nearly forgot to list for the teachers who really teach all the vocabulary words we learned and used:

HIAWATHA WORDS	EVANGELINE WORDS	STANDISH WORDS	WAYSIDE INN WORDS
legend	primeval	matchlock	repose
reverberation	prophetic	diligent	weir
eyrie	disconsolate	azure	wainscot
plover	roe	scribe	spinet
grouse	shuttles	skirmish	lament
alders	matrons	arsenal	uncouthly
palisades	prevailed	adage	latent
comprehend	stalworth	invincible	attire
efface	congregation	pillage	virtue
inscription	woodbine	logic	chronicles
crag	wains	intermingled	supple
quarry	penitent	averted	peruse
chafe	eaves	prominent	aspect
tranquil	odorous	consolation	fastidious
hereditary	suitor	epistles	cataract
compassion	pedagogue	memoirs	aromatic

HIAWATHA WORDS	EVANGELINE WORDS	STANDISH WORDS	WAYSIDE INN WORDS
defiance	crevice	immortal	sprites
abyss	expired	elegant	avail
brant	valiant	taciturn	grenadiers
wranglings	abundance	wooings	stealthy
dissensions	inclement	dismay	kindled
discord	consoled	maxim	steed
calumet	russet	discreetly	spectral
cumbrous	distended	populous	aghast
smote	ponderous	impious	gauntlets
derision	tassels	anthem	grave
dominion	udders	ravenous	cavaliers
caresses	peals	pallid	rouse
cormorant	pewter	encumbered	perchance
fens	flax	quailed	purveyor
indolent	jovial	blurted	pompous
asunder	accustomed	dilated	eddying
sinews	embers	zeal	falcon
tresses	mandate	placable	reveries
haunches	blighted	magnanimous	centennial
palpitated	dubious	perplexed	trellises
exulted	scythe	apocalyptical	mute
lore	besieged	turrets	exhilaration
enchanted	notary	grottos	suffused
portals	guile	mutable	disdained
lurid	demeanor	transgression	rustic
vapors	irascible	abasement	bergamot
awe	presided	contrition	cloves
perilous	corrupted	cordage	pursuivant
indomitable	scaffold	bondage	anticipates
invulnerable	congealed	kindred	intensified
prowess	comment	sombre	villa
benignant	brazen	martial	commend
related	tankard	demolished	injudicious
hoary	infinite	minutely	stagnant
remorseful	luminous	wrath	noxious

HIAWATHA WORDS	EVANGELINE WORDS	STANDISH WORDS	WAYSIDE INN WORDS
assailant	tremulous	hostile	manifold
tumult	jocund	scabbard	abate
valor	alternately	abashed	vespers
jasper	sonorous	dexterous	seditious
chalcedony	dissonant	indignant	mire
blithe	sultry	pedigree	effulgence
haunts	solstice	chrysolite	impostor
rivulet	imprecations	importunate	boisterous
exertions	rebuke	choleric	motley

We learned more than 60 new words in each Longfellow masterpiece. My boys and girls understood these words because they were learned in the context of genuine emotions in great writing.

"Hiawatha," "Evangeline," and "Courtship of Miles Standish" are works that are read all over the world but not too often in elementary schools. My critics say these poems belong in the high school, not the elementary, but I say, "Wrong again!" There's not a high school kid today in America who would accept the antics and actions of a Hiawatha; there's not a high school kid in America today who would accept the traipsing of Evangeline from Canada to Louisiana, to the Ozarks, and to Philadelphia for her Gabriel. Elementary school children today are sophisticated and are willing and able to tackle Longfellow's tales.

The classroom English or language arts teacher is the watchdog of great literature, and it is our job to see that students are exposed to the words and thoughts of great writers, even if the community is indifferent or the school principal not fully aware of their importance.

In the Longfellow Lab there were no tests and no grades. We just shared moments of nobility handed down to us by Henry Wadsworth Longfellow.

The poetry of Longfellow's "Hiawatha" fascinated me. I repeated the words over and over at home just to hear their marvelous rhythm.

Kathy Hruby, 1965

I still have my mural of Hiawatha ascending into the heavens. I'll always remember how much fun it was taking the murals to the other classes and explaining the poem. The painting of the murals helped me develop my love for art.

Robin McLeod, 1963

Trips Without Mama

WHETHER IT BE ROLLER SKATING with a dozen fourth-grade girls or escorting seventy-six fifth- and sixth-grade boys to a hockey game at Madison Square Garden, an elementary school trip is an adventure.

One year my St. Luke's School sixth-graders went to Washington, D.C., to explore that city. We did not discuss and analyze every phase of Washington, D.C., for months in advance; we just decided that seeing Washington, D.C. would be fun. Some of my colleagues have said, "Fun, fun, fun — phooey!" However, I can never do anything unless it is fun.

We went by bus very early in the morning, something like 5 a.m., and returned very late that night. We certainly saw Washington, and even bumped into the late Senator Estes Kefauver in the Senate hallway. He did not have time to give us his autograph, but he did unofficially welcome us to the Senate. This unscheduled incident gave the group a warm feeling of acceptance.

The Potomac River, Mount Vernon, Robert E. Lee's home, the whole of Washington, was included in our unplanned trip. We hunted around and found a bus company that gave us a good monetary deal and happily discovered that the bus driver liked talkative children. He shared with us the Washington he loved. It's impossible to plan such a curriculum in advance.

The phase of the Washington trip I remember best was when my group of twenty-five hungry students entered a restaurant for lunch. The waitresses flung up their hands in dispair as they imagined their domain being plunged into chaos. With considerable self-control I ignored their antics.

The children sat at various tables and ordered with a minimum of confusion. Spaghetti or hamburgers were their main choices. By dessert time the waitresses were more relaxed as they observed that the children conversed, smiled, and politely asked for more bread. Only one spilled his water. When we left the restaurant, the waitresses were beaming, for my twenty-five students had discussed among themselves how much they should tip, and they were far more generous than their teacher.

The waitresses remarked that mine was the best group that had ever come and asked us to please return again. I remember the restaurant affair with much more detail than any other event of that day because there were twenty-five children who had not even noticed the distress of the adult world or the later approval of the adult world. Children instinctively do the right thing when given the opportunity.

We were a tired group when we returned to Greenwich Village, but what an adventure. It was a trip of exploration and incidents, with each child taking care of himself.

The following year my sixth-graders went to Boston. We went by train, and we conquered the Hub City.

I shall never forget the policeman who stopped traffic to allow all twenty-two of us to stand on the exact site of the famous Boston Massacre, the sexton who removed the altar railing so that we could say we stood on the altar floor of the famous Old North Church, and rushing to see the famous glass flowers before the Peabody Museum closed its doors.

But the greatest excitement occurred when we climbed Bunker Hill Monument. This may not seem much of a challenge, but it certainly is when the steps of the monument are covered with ice and there is no railing. We helped each other, and we succeeded. In the excitement of climbing Bunker Hill Monument we recaptured the tensions of the American Revolution. True, there were a few scraped shins and torn stockings, but there was also a comradeship that will never be destroyed. Isn't that really one of the most important aspects of a school trip?

Before it became too dark we went to see Faneuil Hall, the Cradle of Liberty. The kids were shocked to see such a distinguished building surrounded by fish markets. The smell was overwhelming. What was even more overwhelming to my little group was the possibility at that time that Faneuil Hall would be torn down to make room for another fish market. Ruth was so incensed that she composed a poem pleading for the life of Faneuil Hall and mailed it to the Boston *Globe*. Fortunately, Faneuil Hall still stands. Whether ten-year-old Ruth and her poem influenced the decision of the Boston officials I shall never know.

Being an ardent hockey fan, we ended our Boston trip by attending a Boston Bruins hockey game. Some of the girls knew absolutely nothing about the game, but the festive atmosphere engulfed them.

We were not able to locate a bus to take us around to the various landmarks of Boston, but I think we solved our problem in a most unique fashion. The president of the class jumped in a cab with a group of kids, the vice-president of the class hopped in another cab with another group, the secretary of the class squeezed in a cab with a third group, and I managed to hail a fourth cab with a fourth group. Every time we managed to end up at the same historic landmark.

We returned to New York City by sleeper and, of course, everyone wanted a top berth. As a compromise, I agreed to wake up everyone at New Haven to switch berths. However, I was so exhausted that when I opened my eyes, the porter informed me we were in Grand Central Station and that it was 7 a.m. and time to leave.

We were a tired bunch as we approached the mothers and fathers awaiting us at the main information desk. I can still see the mother who had actively supported the excursion flashing us a big smile of success. We had seen Boston and Boston had seen us!

The snappy military parades of West Point fascinated my class another year. We had cruised up the Hudson River by steamer and upon reaching West Point my twenty-three city fifth-graders were overwhelmed by the acres and acres of bright green grass. They looked at me and I looked at them, and even though I knew I shouldn't have said it, I blurted out . . . "Run, kids, run!"

They ran for almost a mile down that green grassy hill and some disappeared from sight, but they all returned. While they were dashing and tumbling down that bright green sward, a groundskeeper appeared and asked who was responsible for all those children running on that grass and, of course, I replied "I don't know."

Just before racing for the boat back to the city, a bit of creative imaginative play entered the West Point scene. While exploring the grounds, some youngsters discovered a Cullum Road. Naturally it was named after my famous general grandfather!

One year I traveled to New York City from Rye, New York, with a group of sixth-graders to see Siobhan Mc-Kenna perform the title role of George Bernard Shaw's *St. Joan.* After the play she welcomed us backstage, and I shall never forget how graciously she handled the group. She told them how much they reminded her of her son who was waiting for her in Dublin.

That particular afternoon Miss McKenna was not feeling up to par for she had a cold, and the combination of not feeling too well and my sixth-graders reminding her of her little boy at home would have landed all of us in Ireland if she had wished just a bit harder.

My students appreciated the humor of Shaw's *St. Joan,* particularly George, for his laughter annoyed an elderly gentleman sitting directly in front of us. "May I remind you, young man, that this is not a comedy," growled the gentleman. I later explained to the children that they were right to laugh, for Shaw intended us to see the humorous side of Joan as well as the serious.

Another year groups of fourth-, fifth-, and sixth-graders went to New York City to see the Old Vic Company of London present *Macbeth* and *Romeo and Juliet.* One group chose to see a Saturday matinee of *Macbeth,* and another chose to go the following Saturday afternoon. The children who saw *Romeo and Juliet* had the delightful experience of the year when they went backstage and had the opportunity to chat with the live Romeo and Juliet. After exploring the interesting set, we sat on the stage floor and exchanged Shakespearean comments. I shall be eternally grateful to the young fellow playing Romeo for becoming so naturally involved with my young, impressionable students. He asked them questions about the plays they were reading:

"Who's playing Mercutio?" he asked.

"I am," replied sixth-grader Bob.

"Who's playing Benvolio?"

"I am," said Timmy as he raised his hand.

Our English actor friend made it a point not to exclude anyone and even asked Carl, our Romeo, if he had difficulty with a certain speech.

The young lady playing Juliet was not as comfortable with the students, but she did chat quietly with Patty, our sixth-grade Juliet. When we left to return to Rye, the live Romeo and Juliet shook hands with each student and wished them good luck with their production of *Romeo and Juliet.*

There have been many museum ventures. The $1.98 reproductions introduced weekly in the classroom prepared us for the thrill of recognizing authentic master-pieces. I have the greatest collection of inexpensive re-productions — that is, after Macys and Gimbels.

At the front door of every museum I gather my students about me and I review the ground rules:

1. Obey all rules and regulations of the museum.
2. You may explore the museum on your own.
3. Meet me at the front door in two hours.
4. Synchronize our watches. "Get set! Go!"

This is really the only way to visit a museum. The method had been successful many, many times until I attempted it in the Museum of Modern Art of New York City.

That particular day Miss Mones and I had combined our classes and were ready to venture forth into the world of modern art, but as our fifty students entered the museum lobby, the guards became hysterical, and the secretary on the main floor would not believe I could be so stupid as to allow a group of children to wander about a museum unsupervised.

Of course the authorities of the Museum of Modern Art won the argument, and we gathered our students and left. Fortunately an ice cream vendor was stationed in front of the museum, and we drowned a bit of our sorrow munching various flavors.

Did the museum officials think the students would deface a Matisse? Did they think the youngsters would push aside an elderly grandmother to see a Picasso first? Did they think the students would make derogatory comments about the hanging of the show? Our particular group of students had voted to share their love of creativity with the Museum of Modern Art but not in the manner of holding hands and marching two by two, stopping at each masterpiece to gasp appropriately. Our classes had outgrown such archaic methodology.

The next day the students wrote strong letters of protest to the museum but in the long run failed to convince anyone that they, as elementary school students, had a dignity that should be respected and a sincerity that should be trusted. However, the museum did send each child a refund.

There are many movies in a city such as New York, and many of them are suitable for the elementary curriculum. The great thing about a movie is to see it on the spur of the moment without too much planning. Just cancel the routine schedule for the day and simply go.

My city students saw Kirk Douglas in *Lust for Life*, Fredric March as Columbus, Claudette Colbert as Cleopatra, and Tyrone Power in *Suez* — an endless list. It was interesting to see another approach to a subject, and there's nothing quite as exciting as to change the pattern of a school day by seeing a movie at 10 a.m. in a practically empty movie house. Eating popcorn and candy were definitely part of the trip.

Many times have I escorted boys and girls to ballet performances and have seen dozens of *Swan Lakes* and dozens of *Firebirds*. The Saturday matinee I shall never forget was the one when a fourth-grade girl started chatting with Hugo Fiorato, the conductor, just as he was about to begin the second ballet. I froze in my second row seat, but Mr. Fiorato apparently was returning the conversation. As soon as the ballet ended, I questioned the aggressive fourth-grade young lady, and the gist of her conversation with Mr. Fiorato had been telling him how much she had enjoyed the first ballet. Mr. Fiorato, a sensitive conductor, sensed the beauty and simplicity of such a compliment coming just as he was about to give the downbeat for the beginning of the second composition.

Every trip I have taken with elementary school children has proved worthwhile, whether they were during school, after school, or on Saturdays.

An elementary school trip without mama is worth ten trips with mama.

And going on trips . . . the trains . . . getting dressed up . . . holding tickets . . . sitting in seats having coats and handbags and eating dinner out. Seeing Siobhan McKenna in Shaw's St. Joan and the Rangers' hockey games and the huge cold rink . . . and screaming . . . and telling the other classes all about it.

Carol Heineman, 1956

I can honestly say that my fifth year of elementary school was one of my most productive, and this can be measured with the passing of years, because I still come across a poem, a famous painting, a vocabulary word, a Shakespearean play, and I remember the countless trips to New York City to see operas and ballets.

Nancy Del Val, 1960

I remember the places you took the class for field trips . . . to hockey games and the circus. I guess what you tried to do was to give us a good education in the classroom and a good time outside where we could burn off energy.

Doug Calo, 1956

Flora and Fauna
in the Gym

WHEN ON THE STAFF of St. Luke's School I wrote a story about a boy named Billy who did not like butter. In fact, he disliked butter so much that he absolutely and decisively refused to eat bread and butter, butter cookies, cake with butter icing, apple butter, and guess what — even peanut butter. As you can see he disliked anything to do with butter.

Billy made life quite difficult for his grandmother with whom he lived, but she kept hoping he would outgrow this nonsensical prejudice.

One morning Billy was awakened by a whir of wings. He rushed to his window, looked out onto his garden, and saw the most colorful, fragile birds imaginable. He rushed into his garden in his pajamas and attempted to catch at least one bird, but they moved too quickly.

"What birds are you," exclaimed Billy. "Speak to me!"

But they ignored him and continued to flit from flower to flower. Billy rushed to his bright red geraniums and said, "Tell me, what are these delightful birds called."

But the bright red geraniums simply shrugged their sturdy shoulders not knowing. Billy then scampered to the friendly waving cosmos and asked, "Where did these birds come from?"

But the friendly cosmos gently waved that they didn't know. The faded pink rambling roses didn't know, the haughty zinnias didn't know, and the asters, the violets, and the poppies didn't know.

The birds were so colorful and graceful that Billy was determined to discover their names. "I know," he said, "I'll ask the old lilac bush. He's been here for years and years and years and he certainly will know!"

Billy ran to the farthest corner of his garden, and there stood the gnarled lilac bush. "Mr. Lilac Bush, what are these birds flying from flower to flower called?"

The old lilac bush pondered and pondered and finally replied, "I don't think they're birds at all. I think they are more like butterflies."

"BUTTERFLIES!" screamed Billy. "I hate butter and that certainly means I hate butterflies."

And at that moment Billy picked up the garden rake and started swinging wildly to drive the butterflies out of his garden. However, the butterflies were very agile and flew away from Billy and out of his garden. But he did manage to strike one tiny butterfly who was just learning to fly. The little butterfly fell to the ground in the center of the garden.

"Come in for your breakfast, Billy," called his grandma.

Billy dropped the rake and went in for his breakfast — without butter, of course.

The hours rolled by, and Billy soon forgot the incident in his garden. The garden was now quiet in dark shadows. Some of the flowers were frightened. There seemed to be a stillness in the air. The little butterfly still had not moved. Maybe he was dead. A strange feeling enveloped the garden.

The brave orange marigolds went to the center of the garden to see if they could help the still butterfly, but it was no use. The moss roses contributed their sweet fragrance, but that did not help the little butterfly. The violets, the snapdragons, and the pansies all helped — but nothing happened.

The garden was now completely black. The flowers were very subdued. "Listen," said the staunch dahlia.

The flowers listened and heard a whir of wings. The butterflies were returning, but this time they were returning with the Queen of the Butterflies. She was beautiful with tremendous wings that sparkled in the moonlight.

The Queen looked at the little butterfly in the center of the garden. He had not moved all day long. She gently stroked his head and fanned him with her huge magical wings. The injured butterfly opened his eyes, and everyone in the garden gave a huge sigh of relief. At that moment the Queen of the Butterflies spoke, "The little butterfly will live!"

She rose into the air with her hundreds of followers, including the injured one, and flew swiftly out of the garden. But as she reached the garden gate, she stopped in

midair and softly said to the flowers, "How can you live in a garden owned by such a mean boy as Billy?"

Off they all flew never to return again.

The garden was now completely dark with only an occasional shaft of moonlight to make life bearable. The little bluebells needed a night light so that they wouldn't be afraid of the darkness. The daffodils were frightened but kept up their courage by huddling their heads together. The small white tulip was crying.

At that moment the tallest sunflower said, "Let's ask the old lilac bush what he thinks we should do."

All the flowers thought that was a good idea, and they rushed to the far corner of the garden. They looked up at the old lilac bush. "In all my years of living in this garden, this is the most difficult decision I have had to make," said the old lilac bush.

There was a long moment of silence. Even the little white tulip stopped crying, waiting for the old lilac bush to decide. The old lilac bush cleared his throat and declared, "I have decided that I can no longer live in a garden owned by such a mean boy as Billy!"

At this point the old lilac bush starting packing his things and so did every single other flower. Slowly they started leaving the garden. One by one they tiptoed out. Billy's garden was almost empty except for a few stinkweeds.

In the morning when Billy looked out of his window, he saw the saddest looking garden in the world. It was empty of flowers! He rushed out to his garden in his pajamas and cried, "Where are my lovely flowers? Where are they?"

There was only a sad silence. But then, a little flowery voice said, "I'm still here."

"Where are all my flowery friends?" asked Billy.

"They left because you were so mean to the little butterfly, but I'm still here!"

"Where did the flowers go?" cried Billy.

"I don't know, but I'm still here!"

"Will they ever come back?" entreated Billy.

"I don't think so, but I'm still here!"

At this news Billy began to cry. He cried big, heavy sobs.

"Don't cry, Billy, for I'm still here. Let me play a game with you. Let me look under your chin."

When the little yellow flower looked under Billy's chin, there was a yellowish glow!

"I knew it, I knew you really and truly liked butter. You see I'm a buttercup, and when I look under a person's chin and there's a yellowish glow, it means that the person really and truly likes butter."

The little buttercup laughed and danced about the empty garden.

Billy was quiet and thoughtful, and then he said, "If it's really true that I like butter, then that means I like butterflies too!"

"Of course," said the little buttercup, "it means that you like butter, butterflies, apple butter, butter cookies, and even peanut butter."

Billy rushed down the road telling everyone that he was no longer a mean boy. He told everyone that he liked butter, which meant he liked butterflies. Finally he became so tired from running and telling everyone the good news that he had to return to his empty garden to rest.

When he reached his garden, it was no longer empty! "We're back!" shouted all the flowers.

There they were all in their regular places, smelling so good and looking so colorful. Every petal was in place. Billy was happy to see them, and the flowers were happy to see Billy. But they weren't completely happy, for the butterflies had flown too far away to know about the new, kind Billy.

The lavender hyacinth said, "Maybe if we wished very hard the butterflies would hear us and return to the garden."

They all wished very hard, but nothing happened.

One lily of the valley had a bright idea, "Let's change the name on the front gate of the garden from BILLY'S GARDEN to KIND BILLY'S GARDEN, and if a butterfly flies by he will read the sign and enter."

The sign was changed, and they waited. Oh, how they waited — one hour, two hours, three hours, four hours, five hours — and then they heard a whir of wings. The butterflies were returning. Slowly but surely the sound of whirring butterfly wings became louder and louder and louder until there they were with their beautiful wings. The Queen of the Butterflies was there with hundreds of her followers, and the slightly injured butterfly was also there with a Band-Aid on his forehead.

Billy and the little buttercup explained what had happened, and the Queen was satisfied. The butterfly with the Band-Aid on his forehead shook hands with Billy, and all was well again.

Every year the Queen of the Butterflies and hundreds of her followers visit Billy's Garden . . . excuse me, I mean they visit Kind Billy's Garden.

When I finished telling my story to the twenty nursery and twenty kindergarten children sitting around me I asked, "How many of you would like the Queen of the Butterflies to visit your classroom?"

Naturally they were all eager to have a Butterfly Queen visit them; I promised them that in a week she would come.

The following week we gathered in the gymnasium. We were all there — the nursery school four-year-olds, the kindergarten five-year-olds, the first-grade six-year-olds, and the second-grade seven-year-olds. All the children sat on the gym floor with their teachers anxiously awaiting the arrival of the Queen of the Butterflies.

Yes, I had found one real live Butterfly Queen . . . well, in my mind she was. She was a St. Luke's School sixth-grader who was elegant, aristocratic, intelligent, creative, and beautiful. She moved very gracefully and had long golden hair. Yes, she was a Butterfly Queen and still is today.

Elspeth danced about the gymnasium with all the primary eyes watching her. This was the beginning of the dramatization of the story "Kind Billy's Garden." There were many volunteers — volunteers to be butterflies and volunteers to be flowers.

One five-year-old couldn't decide what to do, for she wanted to be both a flower and a butterfly. As quickly as you could say "King Solomon," I suggested, "Be a butterfly this week, and next week be a flower!"

"No," said the individualistic kindergartner, "I will be a butterfly in the gym, a flower in my classroom, and myself at home."

A gymnasium floor is a marvelous spacious area in which to work. I'm convinced that all primary dramatizations should take place in a huge gym, or at least a small field, where the children can run and move and experiment.

Steadily our drama developed a structure. Experimental dance steps became favorite routines; some preferred to be talkative flowers, some were strongly silent; some imitated the actions of the Queen, others ignored her. The structure developed as each primary child found a comfortable place within the drama. Each child discovered his or her own level of success.

Finally the day arrived when the butterfly wings and the flower petals were ready. I shall always be indebted to two theater friends, who, for many days and nights, helped me bend wire, cut and paste paper, and splash sequins. It was all for a good cause — the cause of creating a magical world in a gymnasium ruled by an eleven-year-old Butterfly Queen.

The wings were fragile and the petals were fragile, but the children were careful . . . oh, so careful. The Queen had wings almost four feet high attached to her delicate body with very thin wire that would not hurt her royal shoulders.

The audience of children and parents sitting near the walls of the gym was attentively quiet as the drama enfolded. The drama included talking, dancing, singing, daydreaming, and many unexpected incidents.

Remember the part of the story where the little butterfly was injured in the center of the garden and certain flowers attempted to revive it? At the first afternoon performance, little five-year-old Debbie took the part of a gentle violet talking to the seemingly dead butterfly. That particular afternoon she talked and talked and talked and talked. Although she carried on a ten-minute monologue of spontaneous conversation, all the other flowers waited patiently until she had finished. I was behind a screen waiting to turn on a tape recorder for appropriate moonlight music, and I, too, waited for the gentle violet to finish her almost Shakespearean-in-length soliloquy.

There were many moments of true magic in the St. Luke's School gymnasium as the tale of "Kind Billy's Garden" unfolded. There was four-, five-, and six-, and seven-year old magic with an assist from an "old" eleven-year-old grandmother, an "old" nine-year-old Billy, and an "old" eleven-year-old Butterfly Queen.

For months after the gymnasium production, every time Elspeth passed by the primary playground there were five-year-old whispers:

"There she is!"

"That's the Queen of the Butterflies!"

"I was her helper," said a third child.

"She put a Band-Aid on my head," recalled another.

The Queen of the Butterflies will never die in their minds. She certainly hasn't died in mine!

The following year more flora and fauna flourished in the St. Luke's gymnasium. This time there was a cave filled with monsterettes.

The story went something like this. . . . Once a year the fairies of the forest held their annual spring dance in the local forest. However, every year the monsterettes who lived in a dark cave nearby made life miserable for them. The monsterettes chased them and frightened them.

Finally, after years of trying to be understanding and cooperative, the fairies of the forest had had enough. They asked the city soldiers to help them by capturing and arresting the monsterettes.

The city soldiers were very obliging and, when they appeared, the monsterettes ran into the safety of their cave where no one could reach them — or rather people were afraid to go in and capture them.

Should the soldiers enter? They were afraid, but they entered. One soldier stayed outside on guard to capture any late-arriving monsterette.

Soon it began to be dark, and the city soldier on guard duty became worried. He waited and waited, but his fellow soldiers did not come out, and he was too afraid to go in. It became really and truly dark. "What should I do?" thought the city soldier on guard duty.

After much thought he decided to enter the dark cave. Slowly but bravely he crawled into it.

There was absolute silence among the children and the adult audience. It is the silence that comes when children and grownups are really involved, the silence that teachers cherish in their classrooms when everyone is spellbound.

"HELP! HELP!" was heard from the cave.

The little soldier came rushing out of the cave, chased not by dozens of monsterettes, but by one huge seventh-grade monster. You see, the monsterettes had eaten all the city soldiers and had turned into a giant monster.

Now for the battle of the century — the little city soldier, age six, versus a giant monster, age twelve. What a make-believe fight it was!

The audience cheered when the little soldier defeated the seventh-grade giant. So did I.

Working, playing, dancing, acting, making believe in a gymnasium is fun. Something different happened every time we met.

Another flora and fauna gymnasium experience took place at Milton School in Rye with a kindergarten group. However, before becoming active in the gymnasium, I entered the classroom as King Oberon of *A Midsummer Night's Dream*, wearing a velvet cape and a tiny yellow cardboard crown. I described to the five-year-olds the atmosphere of a magical forest ruled by a King Oberon and a Queen Titania. Almost automatically the kindergartners became my subjects — fairies, elves, goblins, and an assortment of woodland sprites. We danced to slow music and to fast music, and we had a delightful time not disturbing the creatures of the forest by talking with our fingers. Even a year later, every so often on the main street of Rye, one of my ex-woodland sprites would talk to me simply through the movement of his or her fingers, and, of course, I responded in the same manner.

In the classroom I introduced Mendelssohn's *Midsummer Night's Dream*, which is so lyrical that they re-

sponded beautifully, gently waving their arms, tiptoe-
ing swiftly around the tables, and then finding a hiding
place in some corner of the room. One time I fed the
youngsters soft, powdery marshmallows so they would
be as light as fairies. The idea seemed to work. I don't
recall the brand of the marshmallows, however.

The children were receptive to my suggestion that
they create their own kindergarten magical forest. We
began by cutting out hundreds of paper leaves of all
colors and sizes and gathering all types of articles to
decorate the trees. As the days went by, the children
brought in string, ribbons, balloons, bags, rope, cellophane, trinkets, cloth, balls, and many other small,
bright objects.

Then we were ready to actually build our Midsummer
Night's Dream forest in the center of the gym. Invita-
tions were sent home to the parents, to other schools,
and to the primary grades of the home school. The audience sat in a circle around the gym, while the kindergartners started building their magical forest before a
live audience. They were very proud as the forest developed.

Our trees were fairly large branches placed in huge
chunks of styrofoam to hold them in place, and all the
odds and ends that had been collected decorated the
dead branches. There were accidents that morning,
when a tree toppled over, but the five-year-old woodland sprites straightened things out.

When the construction job had been completed, I sat
myself at the piano and tinkled out some improvised
soft music. Some of the fairies were very outgoing and
came out of their hiding places and danced about the

gymnasium. When I pounded the keys as storm music they all screamed and went to their hiding places. The program lasted about thirty minutes, and sooner or later every five-year-old became involved and some of the younger guests even joined in.

The kindergartners were so engrossed with building their forest that costumes or even a suggestion of costumes was not necessary. Their everyday clothes seemed most appropriate.

As the program came to a close, a little elf asked the audience to please leave quietly for all the creatures of the forest were sound asleep. "Please do not talk as you leave," he said.

The elves, the fairies, and the goblins played in their forest long after the audience had gone, but then a group of older boys and girls came in for their gym period and we had to leave.

Elementary school gymnasiums make ideal hothouses for creative flora and fauna to grow and develop.

I remember that you played musical notes on the Piano and called out made-up names one or two at a time and we came out doing a fluttering dance. The trees were made out of stickes that had sparkels on them. They were put in cans with cement in them. Some of the made-up names were grasshopper, musterd seed, and Queen Titania. I think that we were dancing Queen Titania to sleep.

Sarah Livingston, 1964

Of course I remember being Queen of the Butterflies. I didn't do much . . . just ran around the gym barely dancing, but the four-foot wings that were made for me all but carried me to the roof. It was magic. I was a scared child and any magic or fantasy I thought about I kept to myself. But when you said, "Come on, you can be a butterfly!" I felt that if it was required at school it must be acceptable at home. And I felt bolder.

Elspeth Woodcock, 1948

Deep in the heart of the forest you could hear little voices and as you crept closer you could see little figures. They would dance and they would sing. They were fairies and elves. They danced around some wood and they spread leaves over it. The fairies had finished their good deeds and now they were at the ring of the elves and fairies. The treat for doing good deeds was marshmallows.

Marianne MacCarthy, 1964

I remember you being the King and calling the elves out of the Magick Forest. I also remember the part where you put marshmallows in our mouths. I also remember the fun of building the magic forest with those big blocks of styrofoam and potted trees. The play was called Mid-Summer Night's Dreem *by shakespeare. Some day I want to see the whole play.*

Tony Elwers, 1964

Beware the Neat and
Quiet Classroom

THE BASIC STRUCTURE was finished — the chicken wire had been cut and attached to the wooden frame, strips and strips and strips of newspaper had been torn, and pots of soupy paste had been stirred to the right consistency. Twenty-six fifth-graders were ready to start building the Trojan Horse.

All the desks had been pushed to one side to give us room to operate. It took us two weeks to build our Herculean horse. We did our regular school work too, including drills in all the basic skills, but there were sporadic moments of free time when individual students could slap sloppy strips of paste-covered newspaper strips against the chicken wire frame. Of course paste did splatter to the various corners of the room. However, the "glory of history" was growing right before our eyes, and a wonderful feeling of accomplishment was swelling in our hearts. Some of the kids worked before school, after school, and during play periods. Occasionally there was a paste fight, but I'm sure the original builders of the Trojan Horse had similar moments of frivolity.

Yes, the room was messy and sticky and had a strange aroma, but we built our horse. There were arguments about how to design and paint the horse, but after a long group discussion, we decided that the horse should be neutral in color, a beige. When our architectural feat was completed, we spent the whole next day in collective admiration and self-praise. There were moments when everyone patted the horse and loved the horse. It seemed immaterial that the room was messy.

Once, after a visit to the South, I returned with two suitcases full of Spanish moss. It seemed an exciting idea to hang strands of it from the ceiling so that each desk would have the flavor of the South as we studied that section of the country. My colleagues referred to me as "Jungle Jim," but my fifth-graders seemed to enjoy the entangled Spanish moss and its little red bugs. The room did become a bit messy with squashed red bugs, but it was only for a week or so until our unit on the South reached its romantic end.

Every Monday morning my twenty-plus sixth-graders pushed back their desks, spread their individual copies of the now defunct New York *Herald Tribune* on the floor, and proceeded to read the morning paper. Of course everyone read the comics first, sports section second, and front page third.

By using adult newspapers I was able to make learning skimming and the value of an index interesting and meaningful. I commuted from New York City to Rye each morning and was able to buy the papers at Grand Central Station. While on the train I composed twenty questions based on that morning's paper, and I arrived at school early enough to ditto one hundred sheets. Each Monday my four sixth-grade classes would see how quickly they could find the answers to questions dealing with finance, war, politics, theater, books, sports, religion, murders, television, and life in general. Each Monday each student would compete against himself to see if he or she could improve his record in finding data.

"Get set . . . ready . . . begin!" The page of questions was flipped over, and the children began to analyze and categorize the questions. They then consulted the paper's index, quickly turned to the proper section, and rapidly skimmed the newspaper pages. Squeals of joy burst forth as answers were found.

Typical questions were:

1. Why did Walter Terry feel the new Balanchine ballet was a great contribution to the world of the dance?
2. Why is the Senator from Mississippi upset?
3. Who assisted Bobby Hull in scoring his record-breaking goal?
4. What did Miss Peach say to Marcia?

I believe Jim held the record of 10 minutes, 13 seconds, for answering all questions correctly.

A dash of excitement is a good way to begin a school Monday morning — or any morning, for that matter. After answering the questions, each sixth-grader would casually continue to read his paper until it was time to change classes. Some finished reading their *Herald Tribunes* at home. It was a pleasant reading episode and a worthwhile one.

True, the room was messy, for the desks were pushed back and newspapers were scattered about, but the experience was productive and, after all, it happened only once a week.

One year each St. Luke's fourth-grader designed and painted his own cathedral. I remember Barry's cathedral was sturdy and non-collapsible, while Joel's was a romantic impression that a gust of wind could have toppled. There were all types of cathedrals, and all were emotionally sound.

The Sisters and clergy of St. Luke's Chapel were invited to vote for their favorite cathedral. One Sister found it difficult to make a decision, so we added another category for the judges, "Which cathedral is the most holy?" About twelve completed cathedrals were scattered about the room, and blobs of semi-dry poster paint spotted the floor. The room was messy, but one thing in our favor was that it was a "holy mess!"

The best way to truly appreciate a da Vinci fresco is to build and paint one. Slats of wood, chicken wire, gooey cement, trowels, brushes, and paints were accumulated and prepared for one fourth grade, and the children went to work with a vengeance.

Earlier the children had submitted many sketches for the fresco, and the class had finally decided to do the scene of the Last Supper. Perhaps they were influenced by the fact that the original da Vinci fresco in Milan was slowly fading away. Our version of the Last Supper, of course, was very different.

In creating a fresco one must paint on the cement while it is semi-wet. The children had to work fast for cement hardens quickly, but they finished in time. As when any nine-year-olds are working rapidly, accidents happened, things spilled, and cement landed on the wall rather than on the fresco. They made a beautiful fresco though, about 12 feet long and 6 feet high. When it was completed, it didn't look too much like the submitted sketch, but that didn't matter for everyone in the class had contributed to the "masterpiece" with new ideas, changes in color, and alterations in the positions of the religious figures.

At the end of the school year it was sad to watch the custodians smash our fresco, but there was no alternative. The fourth-grade da Vinci fresco was so large it couldn't be maneuvered out the door and, besides, it weighed a "ton." Our fresco was so durable that heavy sledge hammers were required to destroy our cultural contribution to the school.

Murals galore are painted in classrooms; class newspapers are collated; costumes are prepared in the backs of rooms; Greek friezes are created; hundreds of paintings are mounted for annual outdoor art shows — all these activities add to the mess. To me, however, messy classrooms are perfectly natural if something is happening in that room. If dreams of greatness are to be fulfilled in elementary schools, I don't see how teachers can avoid having messy classrooms. Sometimes a neat classroom is a bore.

Don't be upset if you receive a notice from the powers that be that the custodian will not clean your room for the next three days or "Until you get that classroom in some sort of order." On second thought — most of the time a neat classroom is a bore!

I'll never forget the Trojan Horse. The building of that horse was some undertaking. We all took pride in being part of this.
                                                              Janice Germond, 1960

It meant something to me to come to school and to participate in activities besides strictly books.

                                                              Doc Hensley, 1957

Looking around me I find it hard to be out of sight of some of several mementoes witnessing to your effect on our family and myself—whether it is the Picasso hanging on the living room wall, a reading medal on a closet door, or a femur from your science class ornamenting my book chest.

                                                              Bill Kappus, 1960

Hallway Hoofbeats

IT IS STARTLING to hear noise in an elementary school hallway, but it is even more startling to hear the sound of hoofbeats in an elementary school hallway. What was more startling was to see cardboard horses being ridden by a group of live pilgrims heading for Canterbury. And what was most startling was that these live pilgrims were nine-year-olds in the fourth-grade.

The excitement of Geoffrey Chaucer's stories swept through quiet hallways with the horses neighing, swaying, and prancing. Those nine-year-olds didn't actually go to Canterbury, but they relished some of the most famous tales in the English language, Chaucer's *The Canterbury Tales.*

Many years ago people in England went on four- to five-day trips to Canterbury for religious reasons. To pass the time they told each other stories, and the one who told the best story won a prize at the end of the trip. One particular group of pilgrims traveling to Canterbury included Geoffrey Chaucer, a knight, a squire, a wife of Bath, a yeoman, a prioress, a summoner, a pardoner, a franklin, a manciple, and other such interesting folk.

Our trip to Canterbury started one day when I could no longer stand the fourth-grade basal reader with its middle-class stories and its middle-class workbook. For example, I sensed the dullness of an artificial story about a group of kids who formed a club, which stressed group action over individual action. Children know the importance of the group, the importance of parents, Christmas fun, working on a farm, being a baseball star, and so forth — schools should give them other values too, such as a touch of grandeur, a touch of nobility, and a touch of greatness early in their lives. It might make all the difference!

To me it seemed natural to rewrite some of the Chaucer stories and use them as a basic reading series. The material was challenging and stimulating for the students. The class and I placed ourselves back in the 1300's and read about Palamon and Arcite as told by the knight. The mystery of the Loathly Lady was just as tantalizing now as in the days of King Arthur. Everyone was touched by amazing Griselda in the story "Patient Griselda." The ironic justice of "The Three Thieves" was wonderful enough to read again and again. "The False Alchemist," "How the Crow Became Black," "The Calamities of Constance," and others made our reading program one that had some dignity. It was like reading *The New York Times* each morning — the stories were varied, rich, and detailed.

Hoofs beat in the hallway as the children pranced to other classrooms to tell a Chaucer story.

The art department was so busy teaching basic skills that it could not help us make our cardboard horses, so we made our own Canterbury horses. A horse consisted of a cardboard box into which a child stepped. A head, some reins, a tail, and a dash of poster paint were applied to the box, and the nine-year-olds were ready to head for Canterbury. In one day they constructed twenty-five horses!

In attempting to "ride" the horses, some of the boxes fell apart, but quickly and without discouragement students helped each other put the horses back together again. There were all levels of creative achievement, but each rider was most attached to his or her own horse. Naturally we sacrificed certain curriculum-structured subject matter that day, but I'm sure ours was the only fourth-grade class in America planning and starting a trip to Canterbury, England.

Our original plan was to travel to other schools in the system. The kids were most willing, and it would have been quite an experience for them to walk or trot their horses about the city, but the administration felt the plan was too different and would cause confusion. However, we did visit other classrooms in our own building, and the Canterbury pilgrims made a genuine impression. Six-, seven-, and eight-year-olds asked many good, sound questions about our Canterbury tales. My nine-year-olds even had the intestinal fortitude to visit fifth- and even sixth-grade classrooms. It takes a lot of guts to address older students.

Telling a story and adjusting it to various age levels is not an easy task, and by the end of the week as our trip came to an end, the stories were told without too many "uhhs" and "ahhs." The vocabulary of the story-tellers flowed like wine! Not all the kids told stories to others. They all read them and discussed them though, but only the ones who volunteered to tell a story did so.

For a week they practiced in pairs, experimenting with their own class and accepting praise and suggestions from their classmates. It's difficult to be a good storyteller. First one must know his subject matter thoroughly, he must make his presentation interesting, he must choose his vocabulary carefully, and most of all the storyteller must have confidence. All this the boys and girls accomplished simply because they were given the opportunity.

Why not go with your class to Canterbury and pick your own prize-winning story? I guarantee you won't regret the trip, and I can assure you that all your Canterbury pilgrims will return safely!

It was difficult at first because the old English was rather confusing, but after reading The Canterbury Tales *over again, I picked up the pattern of the old English style and it became part of me.*

Louise Lipman, 1963

I read solely for story value and was entertained by Chaucer's tales. I was able to get the obvious meaning from the particular stories I read despite the old English.

Cathy Coshal, 1963

Come Share a Play with Us

CHILDREN THROUGHOUT THE WORLD, in school and after school, engage in creative play, and very often their creativity develops a structure. At this point they say to their peers and to the adult world, "Come and see our play!" or "Come and share a play with us!"

When they are ready to present a play, children have two audiences in mind — one performance for their friends and one performance for mothers, fathers, grandmas, and grandpas. Frequently we teachers and administrators do not give them an opportunity to share their creativity, for quite often we are overly concerned about the success or failure of a production. Success or failure are not relevant if the cast wants to share and the audience is aware that they are there to share.

Putting on plays is exciting, and putting on plays involving good literature is sheer ecstasy. This was the thought in my mind when I decided to celebrate William Shakespeare's 400th birthday in 1964 with a festival that involved approximately nine hundred students, eleven schools, and sixteen classrooms in the towns of Rye, Town of Rye, Port Chester, Harrison, and Purchase. Of course there were difficulties, but the spontaneity of the children plus the flavor of William Shakespeare's words gave me the energy to overcome all obstacles.

The School Board of Rye granted me a sabbatical at half pay so I could eat, and the mothers of Rye started the Cullum Taxi Company to transport me from town to town and school to school. It was the most efficient taxi service in Westchester County, and none of these non-professional, but wonderfully cooperative, cab drivers ever left me stranded.

After working with the various classes once a week for seven months, the Shakespeare Festival was launched in April 1964, with both matinee and evening performances of a different production every day for the whole month.

On April 1 at four in the afternoon a group of sixth- and seventh-graders shared a hilarious performance of *Comedy of Errors* with an audience ranging from first-graders to somebody's very aged great-great-grandmother. There was practically no scenery — just a few scuffed platforms — but there was energy, there was comedy, and there was sharing. Miss Morency's first-graders did not understand all of the Shakespearean dialogue, but they were involved in the story, particularly with the antics of the two identical servants, Dromio of Ephesus and Dromio of Syracuse, humorously played by Larry and Peter.

Before each performance I made it a point to talk to the audience in a very informal manner, discussing the play with them and explaining its more subtle moments. For example, in *Comedy of Errors* I explained to the younger set that the best way of keeping the towns of Ephesus and Syracuse straight in their minds would be to think of the stage in front of them as Ephesus and the back door of the auditorium behind them as Syracuse. Also I reminded them that it would be quite easy to associate the back door of the auditorium with Syracuse and the word stranger since they both began with S! And the people of Syracuse *were* the strangers in Ephesus.

The next day, April 2, at Osborn School in Rye, another Shakespearean comedy hit trod the elementary school boards, *The Taming of the Shrew*. It did not star Richard Burton and Liz Taylor but four elementary school sixth-graders. (I attempted to double cast each main character as often as possible; two Petruchio's and two Katharines could help one another.) There was loads of laughing and loads of sharing by the actors and the appreciative audiences at both the afternoon and evening performances.

On April 7, a moody elementary school *Hamlet* was presented. On April 9, the first *Richard III* ever to feature a female in the title role was performed. Susan of the Midland School sixth-grade convinced me that she could make herself ugly and mean enough to be Richard III, and she did exactly that. Her page-boy hair style was just right, but even if she had had Mary Pickford curls, her interpretation would have been a genuine one.

The scenery was scanty, and the costumes were home-made by the youthful Shakespearean actors and actresses. Many a kitchen curtain or a sister's skirt served as a cape. The wooden swords were crude but served faithfully.

The Ridge Street School in the Town of Rye presented a Shakespearean Sideshow, and a sideshow it was, ranging from Shylock's plea from the *Merchant of Venice* to a rousing wrestling match between Katharine and Petruchio from *The Taming of the Shrew*. At that particular sideshow a Mark Antony spoke to a fickle crowd wrapped in slightly soiled sheets. Laughter burst forth when Caliban, the stupid, pathetic monster of *The Tempest* became intoxicated and "nearly" stumbled off the stage.

Perhaps the high point of the Shakespearean Festival for me was Jane's interpretation of Juliet. Jane was a nine-year-old fourth-grader, and a sweeter Juliet one could not find. She understood Juliet on an elementary school level, and that's all an elementary school Juliet is expected to understand. Jane had wanted to play the role of Juliet since she had been a first-grader. She had seen a portion of the play that some of my sixth-graders had presented that year, and it had remained with her. Jane's parents were concerned about her playing such a demanding role, but never once did I doubt that she could be an honest nine-year-old Juliet.

On the day of Shakespeare's birth, April 23, the Olivia Street School of Port Chester, now called the John F. Kennedy School, presented a very threatening *Macbeth*. It was more ominous than any other *Macbeth*, for instead of having three witches we had six fifth-grade witches, and when afternoon and evening performances were counted, the total of witches rose to twelve. Most of the girls obviously wanted to be a witch, and why not!

Every day in one of the five towns there were two Shakespearean performances, and on May 1 the curtain rose for the last time as a group of senior and junior high school students, ably assisted by elementary school students, presented a most comically relaxed version of *A Midsummer Night's Dream.*

About ten o'clock that evening the sharing of Shakespearean plays ended. Many students, together with their parents, had traveled to neighboring towns and to other schools to see the various interpretations. The plays were good, the kids were great, but still, the most important aspect of all was sharing the plays. A play only comes to life when it is shared with a live audience.

The kids in the casts were there because they had volunteered to be there; the audience was there because they had volunteered to come.

I recall a sophisticated parent approaching me backstage and saying, "Mr. Cullum, Johnny Jones' performance was not my idea of a correct characterization for such a classical and established Shakespearean character!"

"You're absolutely correct, Mrs. So and So, but you must remember that the Hamlet you saw was giving you an eleven-and-a-half-year-old interpretation, and that's all we guaranteed."

I could not continue this discussion for long because everyone was rushing to the Midland School cafeteria where a gala end-of-the-season party was held. Not all of the nine hundred children involved attended because many parents thought it was too late to give a party, but it's never too late for a children's party, particularly if the children are accomplished Shakespearean actors.

Approximately three hundred kids did attend. While they ate homemade cupcakes, soda, candy, ice cream, and crumbled cookies, I acted as the master of ceremonies and asked questions, questions based on the Shakespearean plays presented during the festival. Almost everyone became involved as hands shot into the air. The prizes were pairs of tickets to a professional Shakespearean production.

Louise, who had interpreted the role of Ophelia in *Hamlet* and also the first witch in *Macbeth*, was a winner; Roy, who had been in a production of *Julius Caesar*, was a winner; and Arnold, a high school senior, won the third pair of tickets.

The party ended about midnight. All of us were tired, but it was a wonderful tiredness. It was the tired feeling of having shared a whole month of greatness with the genius of William Shakespeare.

I nearly forgot to mention the crowds of people who flocked to the village green in Rye to have a Sing Along with Shakespeare on a Saturday morning, April 25, 1964. The mayor spoke, and many kids volunteered to perform various Shakespearean scenes in an impromptu fashion. We even had a midget clown from the Ringling Brothers Circus doing cartwheels and somersaults to the delight of the primary children.

Thanks to Dr. Joseph Grimes, Jr., then Superintendent of Schools in Rye, the idea of literature festivals did not lie, for he allowed me to begin plans for a World Literature Festival. The World Literature Festival included almost everything except the kitchen sink.

From March 4 to April 13 in the spring of 1965, with the three elementary schools, one junior high school, and one senior high school participating, we jumped from poetry jamborees to Persian and Greek dramas, to Molière, Lord Dunsany, Maeterlinck, Chekhov, Lorca, and, of course, Shakespeare.

The tension of Schiller's *Mary Stuart* mounted as Carmela, who played Queen Elizabeth, prepared for the scene where she is confronted by her Scottish cousin. In a program involving the poetry of the Spanish poet Federico Garcia Lorca, two human fifth-grade horses, Susan and Ellen, majestically pranced around the stage and dramatically vanished into the darkness. The hilarious farce of Carlo Gozze's *King Stag* encouraged much slapstick among the mixed cast of high school and elementary school students, particularly in the case of cooperative Cathy who played the role of the father, stuffed with a pillow and using her deepest possible voice.

I shall never forget the production presented by sixth-graders of Midland School entitled Literary Faces of America, particularly the second half of the program dealing with humorous American poems and songs. Johanna's interpretation of "Little Brown Jug How I Love Thee," in which she slowly collapsed into an alcoholic stupor, is still very vivid in my mind.

Then there were the early birds of Milton School who arrived at 7:30 a.m. once a week because there was no room in the curriculum at that particular school to work on a production entitled Lincoln in Literature. It was difficult for those fourth- and fifth-graders to reach school early during those cold winter mornings, but they did!

The final night of the World Literature Festival a mixed cast presented the exhilarating Molière comedy *The Imaginary Invalid*. The laughter of the young audience made all the difficulties and hard work of presenting a World Literature Festival worthwhile. Here were young people laughing and sharing the words of Molière. Great literature had entered their lives without a vocabulary list or workbook.

There were twenty-one performances — forty-two counting matinee and evening performances — and each one had its own level of success! I think the primary function of teaching elementary school is to help each student find his level of success.

Again thanks to the moral support of Dr. Grimes, the literature festival idea continued, and in the spring of 1966 the schools of Rye presented a festival entitled Sophocles, Shakespeare, and Shaw. The festival this particular school year was limited to three writers, but within this framework we attempted to develop elementary school interpretations and high school interpretations of the same play for comparison.

It was interesting to hear fifth-grade Barbara discuss her interpretation of Sophocles' Electra with high school student Susan. "I would never do the final scene *that* way!" said ten-year-old Barbara.

Joan the Maid comforts a disconsolate Dauphin→

We had three of Shaw's St. Joans: a fourth-grade Vicki, a fifth-grade Nancy, and an eighth-grade Amanda. They were all good, for they all found their success levels.

One of the most important aspects of the Sophocles, Shakespeare, and Shaw Festival of 1966 was the emergence of critical dramatic opinions among students:

"I prefer Shaw to Shakespeare and Sophocles because there never was a dull moment in his *Androcles and the Lion.*"

"I like Shakespeare because he had that certain touch! Who else would have said 'Good night sweet Prince!'"

"Sophocles is too talky for me. I'll take the action of Shakespeare any time!"

These comments were made by elementary school students. What better way is there to become involved than by expressing an opinion?

The Sophocles, Shakespeare, and Shaw Festival had many moments of greatness, particularly eleven-year-old Jimmy's interpretation of Creon in Sophocles' *Antigone,* the Midland School sixth-grade girls giving up their play period to perfect the movements of the Greek chorus, and John and Neil in the all-boy cast of Osborn School's production of *A Midsummer Night's Dream.* I remember vividly Ellen playing Brutus in the afternoon performance of *Julius Caesar* and Cassius in the evening performance — quite a feat for a fifth-grade girl.

The three festivals are over; the applause has faded; many thank you's are owed to the many supporters who contributed printed programs and transportation to rehearsals; but let me end this festival chapter with a portion of a letter from Stephen Lawson shortly before he entered Williams College:

"I remember a dark stage with a single spotlight on the face of Joan the Maid as she desperately fought against giving in to her judges.

"I remember the chanting of a Greek chorus as it recited its tale of tragedy.

"I remember a hot bull ring in which a heroic matador was sung and wept over before his inevitable death, and the lament of the guitar which set the mood.

"I remember Macbeth's meeting with the weird sisters on the heath and the dark thoughts their prophecies inspired within him.

"I remember the figure of Hamlet, brooding in his tower over a murder and an unfaithful mother.

"I remember the wonderful madness of Toinette being comically chased by an enraged hypochondriac in Molière's *Imaginary Invalid*.

"And I remember other things, seemingly small but overwhelmingly important: the moonlight effect in *A Midsummer Night's Dream*; the awful reality of blood on Macbeth's dagger. These things are just as clear as if they had taken place last week. They haven't faded yet, and I hope they never will.

"But what I remember most of all is the excitement generated by every one of the plays I took part in. It didn't really matter whether I got the chance to play Macbeth himself or just a Greek herald. The excitement was always there, coming from the chance to let yourself go and create a new character!"

I think I got the greatest thrill out of reading and acting out the plays. I think one of the most exciting moments of my life was the time when I played the Duchess in Richard III. *Even now I* can remember perfectly my final speech and how I felt walking off the stage. I think the basic achievement of the class was that it taught us to look for the feeling inside ourselves and to express them in as many ways as we could.

Merrily Gerrish, 1961

I really enjoyed Shaw's St. Joan when I played the Dauphin. I felt so free when I did that part. No matter how large or small the audience, each play was a thrill for me. Those few moments before the curtain made me, and I'm sure everyone else in the play, tingle all over.

Jon Lawson, 1966

When I was saying, "Now cracks a noble heart . . . Good night sweet Prince, and may flights of angels sing thee to thy rest!" I had a great feeling going through me. I don't know what it was, but I just felt so great I thoroughly enjoyed playing Horatio. All the performances had real feeling and this kept me from having stage fright or falling out of character. Not even a joke could make me break a straight face."

Claire Moos, 1965

The point I'd like to make is that you scared undramatic little people like me into using a little volume and trying a little Shakespeare on the stage . . . and to my surprise, it was fun.

Susan Henry, 1961

You allowed every actor and actress to expand on their parts as they thought best. I was surprised at how much imagination the kids had when they were allowed to use it.

Kathy Hruby, 1966

I have found that the basic knowledge of good plays learned with you helped me in some of my college courses.

Bill Cornelius, 1959

Nothing So Rare as a
Day in June

WHEN A TEACHER and a class have been living together an entire school year, with touches of greatness plus some sour moments, nothing is so rare as a day in June! The joy comes not from its being the last month of the school year, but from the fact that those precious, quick-silver, pulsating days in June are the days of fulfilling the love that has been present the whole year through. It is almost impossible to live from September to June without developing a sense of pride about one's students. The class becomes an intimate family group with teacher and students aiming for the same goals. Honesty and trust develop between the teacher and his pupils. Of course there are bad days and difficult situations, but all families have such days.

June can be a month of excitement during which all the skills acquired during the year are reviewed. The final month of school should wrap up the year with a feeling of success. What better way to end the school year?

If one of my students is not truly involved in the excitement of the games and contests held during the final month, then some time during the year *I failed* to fully understand that particular girl or boy.

Most of the time June days are hot and sticky and classrooms are not conducive to mental activity or alert thinking, but with an aura of competition, the unknown, and a smell of excitement, nothing is so rare as a school day in June. I usually closed my door as screams of excitement swelled into the silent hot hallways, but alas, the windows were wide open. But what's wrong with a few yells, and a few screams, and a few groans, particularly if all these sounds are involved with a review of the year's work?

From my many years of elementary school teaching I have many June memories. I recall vividly my royal spelling families donning homemade cardboard crowns while waiting to see who would be king or queen of them all. Throughout the year my fifth-grade students strove to achieve six consecutive one hundreds in weekly spelling so they could qualify for the royal spelling family. Almost all succeeded in reaching this goal. For those who qualified, the first requirement was to make as elaborate a crown as possible, and the second was to wear that crown twenty-four hours a day, beginning June first, until a king or queen was determined.

What nobility, what dignity were displayed as the royal spelling family of ten-year-olds wore their crowns to the cafeteria, to the gym, on the way to school and home, to the public library, and at their dinner tables. Twenty-four hours a day they wore them!

Not all the adult world fully grasped the significance of this make-believe royalty. Sometimes grownups attempted to degrade the dignity of the creative children or tried to tamper with the spirit of the young believers, but, of course, they failed. My ten-year-olds proudly wore their magnificent crowns, all made with sincerity and taste, and entered into the excitement of the royal spelling family game. Basically, it was an interesting and different way of reviewing spelling, and quite often we utilized sixth-grade words, seventh-grade words, and even some eighth-grade words in ascertaining a legitimate king or queen.

Having truly lived together throughout the short school year, such a spelling review was pleasant and possible, for the students were supportive of one another. The blackboard was used so the whole class was involved with the reviewing. Each day the following procedure was followed. I dictated the words, and each potential king or queen took a turn writing the word on the board. The class was silent as the word was being written. When a student misspelled a word, off came his or her crown, and it was tacked to the bulletin board. As soon as an elimination occurred, the eliminated student helped friends review. A Margaret would help a Nancy, a Peter would help a Paul, a Debbie would help a Karen, and finally a sovereign speller would emerge upon the scene.

There was excitement, there was fun, and there was the basic skill of learning how to spell, but the feature I liked the best was that the royal spelling family had the dignity to wear their crowns. One day I even saw a cardboard crown on the head of a second baseman completing a double play in a local baseball game. The children of the neighborhood and in other grades respected the individuals wearing the cardboard crowns, even if some of the adult world did not comprehend their significance.

All year long my students were involved with the richness of words, the excitement of words, and the delicacy of words. Classes were divided into four teams, with a captain for each, and words were collected from our literature, from our social studies, from the students' homes, from television, from anyplace. Everyone was eligible to contribute words to our list. The words introduced in my classroom very seldom came from basal readers and their workbooks, for the students had a vocabulary of their own that far surpassed the naive scope of the reading curriculum.

Running vocabulary races about once or twice a week during the school year was a good method of reviewing — and it was fun. That's a word that is essential in all elementary classrooms, particularly in the process of reviewing. There were many teams through the years — The Lightbulbs, The Silver Streaks, The Raiders, and so on.

Each class held its own elimination contest, and its winning team then competed against the winning teams of the other fifth-grade classes. What a day when Campbell's team, The Avid Six, was fighting for the vocabulary championship of the school against Beth's team, The Walking Websters. The auditorium was packed with kids of all ages. The primary children cheered for older brothers and sisters or just friends, even though the definitions of such words as "sinister," "complacent," "abstract," "indifferent," "remote," and "wan," were not completely understood. Admission was free, and everyone was welcome.

At 3:30 p.m. in the Midland School auditorium on a beautiful June day the World Vocabulary Championship took place. Both teams sat on the stage with me. There were five members to each team, and I served as the moderator. Sometimes I would ask a team member to define a word, and at other times I would give a definition and the participants would give me the suitable vocabulary word. Each question answered correctly scored a point, but each question answered incorrectly was a loss of two points. However, if a team member was not sure of the answer, he was allowed to pass and there was no penalty.

Beth's team took the lead and forged ahead. It looked as if Campbell's team was completely outclassed. The knowledgeable audience was surprised, for Campbell's team was the favorite to win, based on its previous performance during the school year. The first half ended with the score: The Walking Websters, 18 points; The Avid Six, 7 points.

After a ten-minute intermission, the second half of the competition began. It seemed a hopeless situation for The Avid Six until the moment Campbell's mother entered the auditorium. She had been delayed, but her entrance seemed to inspire The Avid Six team. With determination and concentration they forged ahead, and the final score was: The Walking Websters, 30 points; The Avid Six, 32 points.

The auditorium was in an uproar with cheering. Beth and her team sincerely congratulated The Avid Six, and a new World Vocabulary Championship team was heralded in Westchester County.

Year after year former students taking entrance exams to prep schools and colleges have commented on the value of encountering challenging words in the elementary school. They felt comfortable with the reading comprehension sections of their entrance exams and used good sound words when being interviewed.

Learning the basic skills of arithmetic is an essential task for each grade level, and to make learning these arithmetical skills a pleasure is also essential. All year long my classes worked hard to understand and perfect arithmetic skills. We organized speed races, marathon races in which we would spend the whole day working on arithmetic skills, and other types of games to give variety and interest to the subject. Then on a rare day in June students entered the fifth-grade Arithmetic Olympics to see if they could win an Arithmetic Olympic medal.

We had an addition champion, a subtraction champion, a multiplication champion, a division champion, a fraction champion, a problem-solving champion, and an introduction-to-algebra champion.

There was much dashing about the room as children ran up to my desk to have their work checked and then ran back to their seats to tackle more difficult arithmetical obstacles. If their answers were correct, they could proceed to the next example, but if they did not have the right answers, they had to find and correct their errors.

The first three students to finish the ten examples received points, and the first student to acquire a certain number of points became the champion of that particular area. Everyone loved this exciting and enjoyable way of reviewing. It's fun to be an arithmetic champion on a rare day in June.

A touch of greatness that I consider essential in all elementary classrooms is introducing art masterpieces of the world. All year long we enjoyed paintings ranging from impressionism, to surrealism, to realism, and even abstract and primitive with a dash of pop art. We never dissected or analyzed the masterpieces. I would explain briefly a particular style, but mainly we spent our time guessing the titles of pictures and observing the paintings for about a week. It was interesting to see opinions change.

On a rare day in June, fifth- and sixth-graders were prepared to recognize artists through the style of the paintings. About fifty reproductions were tacked about the room, and armed with pad and pencil, the students studied each painting carefully and identified the artist, the school of painting, and the title. Identifying the artist correctly was worth three points, the style of the painting two points, and the title one point.

Each child took home a reproduction, and the student with the most points had first choice, the next highest had second choice, and so down the line. It was unfortunate when just before his turn, someone's favorite painting was picked by the person just ahead of him. However, quick compromises were reached. After the art auction exchanges were sometimes made, and students went home happily with a "masterpiece" tucked under his or her arm.

I still can see Andy with his "Horses in Midstream" by Delacroix, Bob with Klee's "Sinbad the Sailor," Ira with a Modigliani, Bill with Picasso's "Seated Harlequin," and Ann with a Roualt — and that was a painful compromise for she really was a staunch Hopper fan. My fifth- and sixth-graders, whether they compromised or whether they were elated with their selections, were comfortable with the artists and their creations.

Perhaps my favorite day in June was when my fifth- and sixth-grade students gathered in the auditorium to present their readings of poems in the Poetry Finals. Even though I have been involved with Poetry Finals for approximately twenty years, many interpretations are still memorable: Jon's rendition of T.S. Eliot's "McCavity the Cat," Joanne's romantic interpretation of Edgar Allan Poe's "Annabel Lee," Bonnie's delicate phrasing of Robert Louis Stevenson's "The Wind" . . . many, many poems filled with many, many moments of sincerity.

The readings of the poems was based on three things: volume, enunciation, and interpretation. To be absolutely fair in the judging, I invited high school teachers, principals of other schools, and friends to be judges.

Whether my students became poetry finalists and eventual winners or whether they had been eliminated ing the quarter and semi-finals is basically unimportant, for they had romped with poetic phrases and had lived with poetic thoughts. My elementary students were not embarrassed by the love expressed by poets but rather seemed to join them.

I have been extremely fortunate to have shared so many June days with so many, many students. The empty hallway shortly after the last day of school, with the one sneaker in a half-open locker, reminds me just how fortunate I have been.

Nothing is so rare as a school day in June!

I remember that we were always excited and always had more work than the other classes. We felt rather elite with our crowns and our contests in June. What a fantastic month!"

Lori Heineman, 1960

The "Golden Age" of my education. . . . I remember especially preparing a speech à la Disraeli from extracts of his speeches. We all felt like distinguished senior statesmen for the day. Another project was the vocabulary list we kept and frequently added to, which made us all junior lexicographers and more aware of language — an interest that is very much with me today."

Mark Woodcock, 1949

There was always that excitement. Delightful, contagious excitement. It came up stealthily and grabbed people unawares.

Amanda Birrell, 1964

I can remember that there always seemed to be a great amount of excitement and challenge with everything we did. In order to bring out the creativity within us, you treated us more as intellectual children who could produce rather than just children who had to be taught arithmetic and geography.

Erica Tilts, 1956

Appendix:
Actions and Reactions

Throughout this volume brief comments and reminiscences by former students indicate the reactions of elementary school children to Mr. Cullum's creative and individual approach to education. Five additional letters, which were written to the author and the editor by professional colleagues and students, are reproduced here as further testimony to the significance and substance of Mr. Cullum's teaching methods.

MEETING MR. CULLUM and teaching with him was a stunning influence in my professional life as a teacher. He has had such an enormous amount to offer for so long that it is exciting to realize that some of his ideas and philosophy will finally be shared.

Early in my career as a relatively new teacher I had not yet decided what there was about teaching that I liked, and perhaps I hadn't given it that much thought. But I expected it to be more exciting, more stimulating, more rewarding — more something than it was. But this unsureness was to change.

I remember observing in his class for a short time when I was hired in a mid-semester. The children were doing some work in science. I don't remember the content now, but I do still vividly see the aliveness of his group. I didn't think too much about it at the time except to note that that class had a different feeling from all the others I had observed — it was apparent immediately as I stepped into the room.

I then became involved with getting to know my own group and didn't have much contact with Mr. Cullum or the rest of the staff. Then, during one assembly a few months later, Mr. Cullum's fifth-grade put on a play. It was *Julius Caesar*. I was astonished and terribly moved. It was as if I had been unconscious in my work before. I had never seen children so engrossed in what they were doing, so unselfconscious . . . and they were sincere in their efforts. The excitement was communicated to me. I wanted to know Mr. Cullum and how he worked with children. What was he doing? How did he reach them and manage to release such enthusiasm?

Over the next six years I began to find out. It appeared to me always that the children in his room had a totally different air about them — they were freer, more relaxed. This is saying something, because they got to him after five years of "Keep quiet!" Quiet was the prevailing idea of a successful and well-functioning classroom and school. One of the English teachers had up in her room a picture of a hooked fish with a caption something like, "This is what happened to the fish who opened his mouth" — strange notion for a so-called language arts program where communication is the goal.

There was excitement, noise, and laughter coming from Mr. Cullum's room — and hard work! The teacher in that room was no unapproachable authority. The barriers between teacher and student were down.

One year the school grouped most of the difficult children in one bunch and gave them to Mr. Cullum. I believe he asked for them! That year this same group put on Shaw's *Androcles and the Lion*. Not many would have believed them capable of handling the script or the disciplined work required. Poor readers struggled and got help from Mr. Cullum and from each other. And they knew their reading difficulties wouldn't keep them from getting juicy parts. The poor students didn't become geniuses and the problems of the more troubled youngsters didn't disappear, but for some it was the first time they were able to work with any degree of self-confidence . . . and their academic performance improved. For the first time they experienced a little pride in what they did. They had a teacher whom they could talk to and who would talk to them. There were no taboo subjects. He wasn't to be shocked. A marvelous quality was his rampaging sense of humor. He wasn't afraid of appearing absurd before the children. He was willing to reveal himself to them, and they would reciprocate. They were able to share emotionally. Along with this was his attitude of dealing honestly with children, never attempting to mold them to some predetermined cast, supposedly for their own good.

He entered the child's world. I think here was the secret of his communication with them. Their fantasies and fears were not strange to him. Unfortunately, as we grow older most of us lose touch with what is important to children. We become wrapped up in seeing that they succeed . . . on *our* terms. Children are very early hampered by fears and pressures imposed by us, their parents and teachers. Corruption sets in when they begin to see they can get by with charm and hot air. Some are so crushed by failure, they don't even develop the subterfuges — they just fail.

He felt also a wrong focus was set by giving grades. Of what value is it to fail a first-grader in reading? It can't help him read any better; it can only tell him he's a failure. For a short time Mr. Cullum conducted a language enrichment program. It operated without grades; it worked well with many children. They read books and plays, performed, discussed and argued, and wrote voluminously. Most of them did a great deal more work than they ever did under the "requirements."

Of course, there were clashes. He and his children were people confronting each other, with all the energy that circulates in such surroundings. Some children who had been able to sail through with a minimum of effort and a maximum of praise (usually in the form of good grades) sometimes found themselves floundering. The demands he made of them could not always be met in the typically acceptable manner. I remember kids stalking out of his room tight-lipped and furious. Most of the time (but not always) he got through to a part of them that had not been tapped before.

The anger and fury of some children faced by Mr. Cullum and his demands for honesty on their part stemmed partially from the pain of giving up bogus techniques for success. Filling in spaces in a workbook, spelling twenty words correctly on Friday, writing a composition in beautiful penmanship (with little content) didn't work any more. Oh, the struggles that went on with the apparently helpless who "forgot," "didn't remember," "couldn't do it" . . . all excuses to resist facing themselves.

It should go without saying that Mr. Cullum didn't demand the same from all students, but within their own range they had to give. The struggle became one to somehow reach a core of honesty in the child and to have him begin the movement to independence. After many trials most children found they could trust him and they began to come through. Aside from beginning to work more in depth and spurning easy successes, they began to recite emotionally charged poetry, to write more . . . and about personal things.

The projects Mr. Cullum devised were unconventional and dramatic. I remember especially Parade of Presidents, where libraries were denuded of books on Presidents and their times. I still recall the Presidents' speeches before Congress and the excitement of debates. Talk about research! Who would ever value, "Read the chapter and answer the questions at the end" after this. Another was the Royal Spelling Family proudly wearing their crowns and the coronation of the queen with music and the admiration of her subjects. Picasso's birthday was celebrated with dozens of prints hung throughout the corridors of the school; it became a gallery where children strolled and commented. There was *Chatterbox,* the school magazine with its reporters and deadlines, the desks pushed back to collate and staple the many pages of each edition. There were poetry readings after school, with the auditorium filled with children from first through sixth grades, the little ones not understanding all the poems but thrilled to be part of it. In the dance club girls moved on the stage caught up in the rapture of the music and their own movements. One year boys asked if they could join. Only boys who knew Mr. Cullum were able to find the guts to do interpretative dancing with a group of girls. Then there were the hockey teams, where there was room for any kind of player — Al out on the field with a crazy hat running around refereeing. And the plays — they were the vehicles for the most exciting release and feelings of grandness.

All of these projects — and there were many, many more — were marvelous! Certainly one reason was because of Mr. Cullum's many deep and varied talents. He brought these to the children. But I don't believe these were the determining elements in his magical relationship with youngsters. He knew the joy of children in pretending, in drama, and in excitement. He felt the same joy they did. This is what I mean when I say he shared their world.

In all his projects the main object, as far as I understood it, was to provide a situation where the child could expand. They were never ends in themselves.

The necessary ingredient for success in working with children in these or other projects is not to be another Mr. Cullum — that's hardly possible — but rather to be oneself with children — to let them in. Then new paths will open — as they did for me.

Vita Mones Pavlich, Fifth-Grade Teacher
Rye Public Schools, 1956-1962
Rye, New York
Westland School, 1963 —
Larkspur, California

If you'll stick with me, I'll recollect a couple of pagefuls on fifth grade to give you some idea how a ten-year-old boy viewed Mr. Cullum and his class.

For most people, a blanket of fog obscures the elementary school years, hiding every aspect except the playground and the arbitrary decisions of adults. It's very difficult to see how these years shaped our later lives. My first, second, and third grades are an almost total loss, except for isolated, and no doubt blown-up, incidents and the resulting punitive measures. All I retain from these years is a vague sense of the injustice of the school world. I felt I was being made to atone for everyone else's sins. Although I was the leader of the "hackers," I wanted to be treated fairly. By the fourth grade I was a skeptic — I expected the worst from others. I felt a very real need to justify myself in the eyes of the world.

If the first three years of grammar school primed me emotionally for fifth grade, fourth grade primed me intellectually and athletically for the next school year. In fourth grade I first transferred some of my general discontent with my lot from the uneven distribution of justice to my classroom work. I was not only bored but openly critical of the slow pace of my fourth-grade class. Every morning we had to look up fourth-grade words (words that I already knew, having finished the Hardy Boys the year before) in our fourth-grade dictionaries. We had to syllabify the words, give their parts of speech, and define them. I risked a B by compressing the definitions. My brother Ted was in sixth grade, and while he was trying to teach me some algebra he had picked up, my fourth-grade teacher was telling us that we weren't ready for multiplication tables yet.

During second and third grade I would stand out in the snow and rain to watch after-school hockey. It had been previously limited to the two upper grades, but Mr. Cullum, the hockey coach, broke all precendents and let Britzie Moran and me play, Britzie because he was so big, me because I was so damn persistent. But after-school hockey only made me more restless. I was tired of being a fourth-grader. I wanted to learn multiplication tables and play on the first line of the Rangers.

If fourth grade was the Middle Ages, fifth grade was the Renaissance. I wasn't scared as I entered Class 5A the first day, for Mr. Cullum already knew me from after-school hockey. I'm sure that I had Mr. Cullum as teacher and Mr. Cullum as hockey coach hopelessly confounded in my mind that year, for he brought the excitement of the hockey field into the classroom. Nearly every class activity was calculated to be fun. The primary in-gredient was the understanding we had with Mr. Cullum. He was not part of the unfathomable adult world — he was just Mr. Cullum, full of idiosycrasies, Mr. Cullum, ready to laugh at himself. He couldn't hide anything from us. We knew he was getting bald (Britzie would report on it every day), we knew no earthly power could stop him from going to a New York Rangers hockey game, and we knew he liked us, in spite of all his bluster at times. The classroom was his fief, but he secretly let us know that we were co-shareholders. He was fair. He never sent us down to the principal's office — he just set us in a corner with a dunce cap on and laughed at us, and we ended up laughing at ourselves. But disciplinary problems were relatively rare. Order was not maintained by fiat, but rather by the threat of not having an Arithmetic Olympics or a Vocabulary Game. We no longer conformed for fear of punishment, but instead came to realize that our individual desires converged in allowing Mr. Cullum to run the class as he wished. I began to respect others' rights in the fifth grade.

The carrots that Mr. Cullum held out to us in the classroom rarely lost their attraction. Arithmetic Olympics was my favorite. The rules were specific. Mr. Cullum would give us four or five lines of addition or multiplication problems to work out. We would start together, work one line, and run up to his desk as fast as we could. If the line was correct, Mr. Cullum would check it off, if not he would wave us back to our desks, not telling us where we had goofed. This sequence of events continued until the winners were established, and of course everyone had to finish. The classroom was constant motion, constant agony, and constant triumph. Arithmetic Olympics not only made multiplication fun; it taught us how to operate under pressure and that rules were set up for our own good.

Class 5A had vocabulary books into which we put all the new words we ran into in class and any words we brought in from home. The words didn't rot there — Mr. Cullum threw them three times a week at the four teams making up the Vocabulary League. We learned the words because we'd brought them into class ourselves and because we didn't want to let down our teammates.

In similar fashion, Mr. Cullum made our weekly spelling tests into a competitive exercise. Whoever had the most consecutive perfect tests was the reigning King or Queen, the one with the second most was the Prince or Princess. In June, the present and deposed royal family gathered to decide on the absolute monarch by means of a formalized spelling bee. For one week, those royal personages still left in the competition had to wear crowns *all the time* or risk being restored to commoner status by the high priest, Mr. Cullum. He would cruise around downtown after school, and I even wore my crown at home for fear that he would drop in and behead me.

The Mr. Cullum who allowed us to play classroom hockey and run over each other in Arithmetic Olympics was balanced by the Mr. Cullum who directed the school plays and introduced us to Vincent van Gogh, the crazy man who cut his ear off. He performed the near impossible when he cast the hockey team in *Joan of Arc*. He entrusted me with the role of the executioner, and I misplaced his confidence by skipping one of the crucial three lines I had to spout forth on the night of the performance. We all knew who the actors were, but Mr. Cullum could line us up two-by-two wherever he led.

Fifth grade with Mr. Cullum meant something different to each of us. We felt that we were individuals because we were members of a group. We felt that we were individuals because Mr. Cullum respected our rights, though we didn't always respect his. Saturday and Sunday were but connective tissue between the muscle and action of the school week. For a whole year I never once played sick. School was no longer a duty, like making your bed; it was demanding work and exciting games. It taught me that the pursuit of excellence could be fun. The outside world of adults, books, plays, and art was no longer out of reach. I've built up fifth grade to be a watershed in my life.

> David Pugh, Fifth-grade, 1959
> Freshman, Stanford University, 1966

In many ways Albert Cullum was the most outstanding teacher we have ever had. He made the program so creative and interesting for the children that to many of them it was the first time in their lives they ever waked up to the wonders of the world in which they live. Al's concern was for each individual child and it reached way out beyond the classroom into their home life and the world of sports and everything that it means to be growing up. If I could put in one sentence what seemed to be the most unique aspect of Al's teaching, it was that he gave the children a real incentive to learn and a love for finding out about things. He also had a love for each child. Again and again when the children he taught come back, it is about him that they want to talk. He was a great teacher, and I wish we had more like him.

The Reverend Paul C. Weed, Headmaster
St. Luke's School, New York City

I have found it hard to put what I have done with you into words. It is easy to state things like the vocabulary matches, the unique ways of learning grammar, the endless number of plays I participated in, etc., all of which were great learning devices. But what I find the hardest to say is the most important thing you did for me. You taught me to be a thinking individual. I believe you achieved this in two ways. First by telling me the following quotes: "No man has ever become great by imitation" and "When you are on the side of the majority, it is time to reform." It is important in this world not to become part of a mass, but to formulate my own sound opinions. Equally important is Thoreau's quote that says "If a man does not keep pace with his companions, perhaps it is because he hears a different drummer. Let him step to the music which he hears." I have learned to respect all views, and to listen with an open mind.

The second way you taught me to stand on my own two feet, was by being Mr. Cullum. It seems to me you made a point not to conform to set methods of doing things. You always had a new approach toward things. An example was teaching grammar while wearing surgical masks.

I am sure that the most important idea you got across to me was to think completely by myself, and I thank you for it.

Sincerely,*

Coline Jenkins, 1962

* "Sincerity is the highest compliment you can pay." Another I have not forgotten.

I am glad to hear that *Push Back the Desks* has arrived on the education scene. I feel sure that it will open long-closed doors to learning. Ever since Mr. Cullum came to Midland School and began his program of "personalized" instruction (as compared with "individualized" instruction), there has been a series of innovations in teaching techniques. Mr. Cullum becomes so involved, almost enthralled, in his work that he pays little attention not only to the clock, but to the calendar as well. Once embarked upon a project with the children, he would think nothing of working on the idea until two or three o'clock in the morning.

Mr. Cullum's "Mister Speaker!" was one of his first formal projects here. Teaching history by having pupils personalize the characters involved made the subject alive and motivated even the dullest of the laggards to interest. Mr. Cullum was able to enlighten the imagination of all of the children with his Shakespeare Festival. Sixth- and fifth-grade children Romeo(ed), Hamlet(ted), "outed the damned spot!" to the delight of themselves and everyone who came and went away pleased that their children enjoyed Shakespeare (as they wished *they* had!). Mr. Cullum is talented in many ways and with children he uses all of his talents to great advantage. This *Push Back the Desks* should be in the hands of every teacher who really wants his pupils to learn.

J. J. Collins, Principal
Midland School, Rye, New York